A NEW LIFE

THE SEQUEL TO THE UNEXPECTED TRUTH

A NEW LIFE

T H E SEQUEL TO THE UNEXPECTED TRUTH

OLUWAFEMI SENU

LASALA PUBLISHING HOUSE

Published by Lasala Publishing House 2014
10 9 8 7 6 5 4 3 2 1

No characters in this book are fictitious. It is a true life account. Some names have been changed.

First published in Great Britain in 2014 by
by Lasala Publishing House, an imprint of
Lasala Media Limited

Lasala Media Limited
Suite 27, Waltham Forest Business Centre,
5 Blackhorse Lane, London E17 6DS
www.lasalamedia.org

Lasala Media Limited Reg. No. 08685665

A CIP catalogue record for this book is available from the British Library

ISBN 978-1-907783-09-8

Cover design by Octagon Lab

For
Elizabeth Senu
Mary Pedetin
Catherine Assengone

I dedicate my book to all victims of abuse and those who have suffered domestic violence

I dedicate my book to the self-employed entrepreneurs, world-changers, dream-chasers, every hard worker and volunteers.
Because those who dream to succeed
and those who help others
are my kind of people

Contents

Acknowledgements

I would like to express my deepest gratitude and appreciation to my three mothers: Mary Pedetin Senu, for taking care of me and showing me love; Catherine Assengone, for teaching me how to be a strong man and giving me a chance in life; and Elizabeth Absoede Senu, for bringing me into the world.

I would like to thank Matthew Idowu, my cousin, for taking the pain and humiliation that would otherwise been given to me during the period when Catherine suffered a stroke. I would like to thank M'bembi Babela for her thoughtful words and contribution. Above all, I want to thank my son Josias who contributed enormously to the writing and publishing of this book.

I would like to thank Salvo Caciloppo, my good friend at Sotheby's on Bond Street who I work with, for motivating, supporting and encouraging me during the writing of my autobiography. My appreciation and thanks are also shared with: former Dean of the University of East London's School of Law and Social Sciences, Fiona Fairweather; the University's Employability Manager, George Laurencin; Dr. Nataliya Shiraz, Academic Skills Lecturer and Professor Daniel Briggs for always believing in me, supporting me and helping me to succeed to my full potential whilst at university.

My deepest thanks also go to my family for their support, especially my wife, without whom it would not have been possible to continue writing.

I would also like to express my thanks to all those who saw me through this book; to all those who provided me support, talked over things with me, read, wrote, offered comments, allowed me to quote their remarks and assisted in the editing, proofreading and design.

Last, but not least, I would like to apologise to all those who've had to put up with me over my life and those I've failed to mention. To everyone who has had an impact and contribution in my life: thank you.

Foreword

I was immediately drawn to this book due to my lifelong fascination with biographies and memoirs, especially as displayed in the world of ordinary people. I was delighted to not only find a story of a great personality (Peter) but also pages filled with risk, struggle, love, belief, trump, endurance and miracles. This is a story of a stronger than life spirit that meets his every challenge with a strength greater than any amount of physical weight that can be lifted. What an incredible inspiration his memoir is and Peter's story is worth knowing.

This story of strength and survival by Oluwafemi Senu is written in a fluid of connecting piece that easily allows the reader to paint a vivid picture of the author's life story. This was such a nice easy read that I found it hard to put down. The author is the man with integrity who tells it like it is, makes no excuses and picks himself up and moves on to his next challenge. Childhood traumas, poverty, fatherhood, fame, travel and finally happiness - Peter has survived it all. Readers, young and old, can take something away for themselves from his life story.

This talented author provides his audience with a triumphant biography that his fans all over the world will enjoy. Additionally, anyone who relishes a true life account fled with downfall and deliverance will enjoy Oluwafemi's message that writing not only *saved*, but filled his being.

Dr Nataliya Shiraz, Imperial College London Business School

Preface

Within this book, you will find that the characters refer to me as Peter, but until you start reading, you can call me Femi. Over the course of my life, I'd like to think that I've become more *educated*. Not educated as in degrees and qualifications, but educated as in experienced. I always liked the quote, 'Life is like a camera. Just focus on what's important, capture the good times, develop from the negatives, and if things don't turn out – take another shot.' Perhaps it's because it essentially summates most of my life, or bizarrely compares life to a camera, but the message it conveys is so important. In fact, it's ultimately significant to any success we may have in our lives.

My childhood was severely affected in two ways: the mistreatment I endured and being lied to.

The mistreatment I faced was primarily at the hands of my stepmother. She'd either put sand in the little food I was given, or she'd randomly start hitting me until she was satisfied. To make things worse, I never knew that my mother had died until I was told by a drunken woman I'd never met before at a party when I was fifteen years old. So my aunt, whom I'd come to love as my mother, was never really my biological mother. It came to a point in my young life where I thought: did I have any prospects? Did I have a future?

I dropped out of school at 14 and ran away from home, mainly because of the abuse I received. I then went in search of a job to take care of myself during the time where I lived on the streets for months. It was also during this time that I realised the value of education. My aunt Mary would always tell me how important it was to go to school and how it could help me in life. I remember the day when I went to visit Mary to give her my first salary. I'd promised myself to do it, as I owed so much to her for all she had done for me. When I got there, she began to talk to me about going back to school. As usual, I told her 'someday I'll return to school.' But that day, my response wasn't good enough. That day, Mary made me promise that I would return back to education. Back then, I didn't realise the significance of my promise but today, almost 30 years later, I do. Funnily enough, that promise snowballed into my ambition. Both were almost intertwined, and it meant that in the pursuit of my dream, I would also be fulfilling Mary's.

Many children all over the world face abuse. Under the blanket of discipline, many parents repeatedly hurt their children. Some do it out of anger, others simply because it makes them feel better. But no matter the case, abusing your children - in fact, abusing anyone - is not right. In my life, it was the catalyst that caused me to leave home. Some will say that in the end it brought me to a better life, but it also shattered my childhood. At a young age, it didn't matter if I was going to find myself in North America, West Europe or East Asia; I just wanted parents who loved me equally. Unfortunately, it wasn't like that.

That's why I work voluntarily with a charitable organisation to make sure that those children who suffer the same childhood experiences I did no longer have to. My contribution may be a small amount in proportion to all the people in the world that work so hard to help young people, but that's one more contribution in the world. There are people just like me who have suffered a similar experience or much worse. But many don't have the opportunity to share it with people. That's why I believe that my story can be the voice of the voiceless and encourage others to share their experiences. Sometimes, it can feel like you're all alone in the world, but knowing there are people just like you can help a lot.

But placing the abuse I experienced behind me, I focused on more important goals in my life: education. I'd like to tell you more about my adulthood, but that's for you to read and find out.

Ever since I was a small boy, I believed that pursuing a dream meant you had a direction in life. Sometimes, you'd never know how you'd get to the end, but you always knew where you were heading to. I never knew that I would become an *educated* man, but I did. And I touched my dream too…

So, it is with great pleasure and much happiness that this book, *A New Life*, is put between these covers.

Introduction

Losing your mother in the first year of your life; running away from home because your parents mistreat you; growing up on the streets of Lagos in a country where poverty is pervasive and then daring to dream big principally describes my childhood. A lot of people say that you should always treasure your youth, so when you grow up one day and you're a man, you can look back at your experiences and say, 'That was awesome!' But what happens when your childhood is ripped away from you and you have to be a man at eight years old? What happens when you sleep in abandoned vehicles and incomplete buildings in humidity, in fear of being kidnapped or in fear of death? What happens when you have the courage to run away on a ship leaving your past behind?

A New Life is an autobiography of my adulthood. It traces the story of a fifteen year old boy who believes that a man afraid of chasing his dream is guilty of cowardice into his older adult years. Not only the sequel to *The Unexpected Truth*, which details my childhood, this story is about having the audacity to pursue your childhood dream, having the audacity to stand up seven times after falling six, and having the audacity to survive. Perhaps at this moment, you're confused or unsure about what I'm talking about, but I had a dream. For some, that dream will be small; for others, that dream will be huge. But my dream is neither big nor small — it's unique to me. My life is an explosion of hunger, desperation, fear, uncertainty and accomplishment, and amidst of all it was me: a small man just trying to go to school. I didn't have a plan; I never did. But I knew that if I kept on going towards my destination, and I took a step forward, the once non-existent path would suddenly appear.

A lot of people also say that you should use your youth to prepare your adulthood. Having a good education, setting the right goals, being guided by your parents are all very important to having a successful future. A lot of people take that path — they're the government officials of the world, lecturers at university, or the doctors and nurses who do a great job helping people. But being really successful — not that I'm an expert — means that you have to be prepared to take risks; you've got to be prepared to not be prepared. In many areas of our lives, a mêlée of people will tell us that preparation is the key to success. They'll convince you that their logical or *complex mathematical algorithms* are infallible, using modern day and historic examples as proof. But when was your life always logical? When were our lives ever exactly how we wanted them to be?

There are always challenges and obstacles that confront us every day, but we always attempt to find a way out of our problems. Sometimes it's easy and at other times it's hard. Yet, although I faced exhausting challenges, I continued to take steps forward. I continued on the course of achieving of my dream, and thereby fulfilling a lifelong promise.

At this point, you'll now be asking yourself: who is this man? My name is Oluwafemi Senu. I am a black, middle-aged man of Nigerian origin living in London. I was born in Ebute-Metta, a suburb of Lagos State. I lost my mother on July 23, 1971. I lost my second mother on an unknown day in November 1997. I lost my third mother on December 15, 2013. I represent a man who has come from a background where leaving intergenerational poverty was essentially thought impossible, but I represent *the* man, like so many others, who will not — even in the worst of circumstances — give up.

That is who I am: a slave of determination.

If you can't fly then run, if you can't run then walk,
If you can't walk then crawl, but whatever you do
You have to keep moving forward.

~ MARTIN LUTHER KING JR

To accomplish great things, we must not only act,
But also dream; not only plan, but also believe.

~ ANATOLE FRANCE

There are those who look at things the way they are,
And ask why…I dream of things that never were,
And ask why not?

~ ROBERT F. KENNEDY

Chapter 1: The Groaning Wails of Men

My thoughts drifted. The immense sadness of my trials permeated my heart and gradually leached into my mind. I could no longer continue to suffer the torment. My plea for help was my last resort, but even I knew it was meaningless. The long journey towards the Port-Gentil Gendarmerie allowed me time to soak in my worries, fears and anxieties. What had I just done? It was too remarkable to allow the thoughts to run in my head so I simply avoided them and gazed out of the window of the small vehicle, knowing that the next few moments of my life would perhaps match the ordeal I had only experienced a few hours ago.

We exited the small vehicle, and slowly walked into the relatively small Gendarmerie. The officer removed the handcuffs from my wrists once we were inside. I felt a surge of relief. I looked at my wrists; the dark ring lines around them easily noticeable. They were aching with severe pain, but my hands were once again free.

'Where are your papers?' shouted the commanding officer at the Gendarmerie.

I gave no answer. My silence caused not by my will to ignore, but my inability to convey speech. I simply watched as Yanke and Texan sluggishly revealed their travelling papers. My heart sank. The only proof of identity I had was my birth certificate. A thought ran through my mind — would this suffice?

I was beaten. Again... and again... and again.

Blood was splattering on the walls; my flesh was open; the wounds stinging. I knew this would happen; I had only hoped the pain wouldn't. But who was I kidding? It was unbearable. Every hit of the baton not only struck my body, but my heart as well and I looked to the heavens for mercy.

About five hours later, we were taken to a dark cell. En route, I was handcuffed with Texan, while Kofi was paired with Matthew, and Yanke was handcuffed alone. I winced as the handcuffs were placed on my wrists again. The cell was small, damp and cold. It was less than two meters from every side and was certainly not suitable for an animal to stay in, let alone five men. The cold, silent walls seemed to remind me of every bad thing that had happened in my life; I'm not sure whether the gendarmes knew that this was torture in itself.

We were all unable to sit down or settle our heads at the same time, as there was simply no space. Handcuffed together in the cell, we were like caged animals. We arranged relief times amongst ourselves; we were each allowed ten minutes to sit down, whereafter we had to stand.

Despite the strains, aches and pains that punched our bodies, we were not spared the merciless beatings of the Gabonese gendarmes. Every so often, a certain gendarme would enter our cell with a small wooden board, its size about $10cm^2$. He was of average height and build, with a dark face and wrinkled forehead. His back was ever so slightly arched that it could be noticed and his look was rather imposing. His wide nose gave him the stark look of an African man, but his puffy lips accentuated it further. He was very quiet amidst his peers in the Gendarmerie, but his silent persona was unfounded when he came in to beat us. This man was inhumane. He would instruct us to take off our clothes and hold out our members, which would be placed on the small wooden board for him to strike repeatedly, inflicting perilous pain.

Our last meal had been in the evening of our second day at the Gendarmerie. It had now been over a week that we had been in the hands of the Gabonese gendarmes and it didn't look as if we were going anywhere quickly. I looked at the small clock opposite the cell door: 3pm. My stomach pained and I groaned in anguish. For over a week, not even a crumb of bread had passed my mouth. We were weak and you could see it. Our bones were now visible, our bodies hammered and our hope fading. Even the air boasted in its strength against us, whistling away in the background and pushing us about in the cell.

My eyes closed.

I felt a tapping on my shoulder. It was Texan.

'Wake up, wake up!'

I looked up with squinted eyes, unaware of what the time was and wondering what insolence would cause Texan to wake me up from my escape.

'Hello,' the voice said. 'My name is François. I am your friend.'

'Wake up!' Texan was tapping me furiously.

I lifted my head and opened my eyes wider. It was a Gabonese gendarme. François was a tall, young man. His stance was rather authoritative, presenting boldness about him. His face was not dark like the other officers and the light shone on his face, protruding his warm smile. His eyes were constant and shining; their warm energy ignited hope in my weary mind.

'I am not going to strike anyone,' said François. 'Do not be alarmed.'

He opened our cell and pulled us out. As I stepped out, I realised that we had been in the cell for far too long. The cell had begun to reek with a foul, pungent smell. But I only noticed the difference as fresh air slapped me. François removed the handcuffs from my wrists. I breathed, though not of relief; nothing could relieve my grief.

I gazed up at the clock on the wall: 8pm. Suddenly, a thought came over me. I watched François as he removed the handcuffs from Matthew's hands. I calculated the time it would take for him to remove Yanke's handcuffs, how long it would take for my legs to fall beneath me and the distance I had to run. I could make it, I thought. I was out of my mind, but I could do it. As I was about to begin my sprint, François turned around.

'Just in case any of you are thinking about running away,' he chuckled. 'You'll not go very far before I catch you.'

They all laughed. I silently whimpered.

It was coming around to 10pm when François led us into a passage. He told us to sit on the benches located by the walls and gave us something to drink. I guzzled the drink, disregarding my etiquette and the people around me — the sight of food and drink was music to my ears. A ravenous feeling captured me as I began to shove the bread and sardines François gave to us into my mouth. We were given plenty to eat and I was satisfied.

We were surprised to see how friendly François was, especially since all the Gabonese gendarmes we had encountered since our arrival had been merciless. But François was different. He sat with us, ate with us and smiled with us. His English was good enough for us to communicate and he treated us like gentlemen. We thanked him greatly for what he did. He chuckled and promised to visit us the next night. Most importantly, he told us that we were going back home. I smiled at the thought — even going back home was better than the hellhole we were in.

I looked up at the clock; the time was now 7am. We had been up for the whole night and sunrise had just begun. François would soon be finishing his night shift. He handcuffed us again and led us back into our cell. Before departing, he looked at us.

'The commanding officer of the Gendarmerie is my in-law,' he said. 'I'll speak to him. At the end of the day, you're not bad guys.'

François left us, but I wished his shift hadn't ended.

Soon after François' departure, his colleagues began to arrive. We acted as if nothing had happened and began groaning. The gendarmes merely walked passed our cell to and fro. Three hours later, we began to hear François' voice again but he didn't approach our cell. About thirty minutes after he arrived, we were visited by a gendarme. He quickly opened our cell, pulled us out and before we could realise it had removed the handcuffs from our wrists. We quickly realised what had happened.

'Guys,' Yanke spoke joyously. 'François has spoken to the commandant.'

Soon after, we were visited by the commanding officer of the Gabonese Gendarmerie. He was a small man. Like the other gendarmes, he wore black trousers and a short-sleeved light blue shirt. He wore a black kepi and his shoes were freshly polished. When he had finished talking with another gendarme he began walking towards us, moving with grandeur. He had an elegance about him and his stern lip commanded valour from his officers, his authority hung in the air like perfume.

He spoke slowly: 'Food will be given to you shortly and promptly. You will then be locked again into your cell. You give us no problems, we give you no problems.

Currently, we are waiting for your deportation papers. When they are ready, you will be informed.'

His voice carried undertones of gravitas and stateliness and it soon became clear that his post was an embodiment of him. After he left us, we were escorted out of the building. The warm air touched my face and I revelled in it. We were taken back inside to eat.

Once we had finished eating, we were then handcuffed and left in our cells — at least the pitiful groaning had now stopped. The day progressed to evening and we were eagerly anticipating the arrival of François. As our blissful thoughts trailed, the sound of his voice guided us back to reality. He had arrived; at least one thing that demanded a smile.

'Bonjour amis!' he exclaimed.

'Bonjour François,' we ecstatically replied.

He quickly said: 'I have spoken to the commandant and after much deliberation he has softened his hand.'

'Thank you,' Yanke said. 'Thank you for everything.'

His voice trailed; the fatigue in his voice evident in the manner in which he spoke. But his fatigue did not undermine the weightiness of his comment.

'Okay, my friends,' François' reply accepted the token of gratitude.

We were all very hungry, and happy to see that François had brought some food along with him. Later that night, François released us from our cell and removed the handcuffs from our wrists. We sat down and watched him as he began to dance. He called the dance Makossa; it was an energetic dance and he urged us to try. The movements brought life to our weary feet, and I had a lot of fun. François was certainly a good entertainer and it showed;

he danced without mistake. In the face of our troubles, we laughed away into the night.

Morning loomed, and François followed the routine of locking us back into our cells. It had now been approaching two weeks in the Gabonese Gendarmerie since we had been caught.

Days continue to pass and François continued to be kind to us. One day, on François' night shift, he arrived at our cell, with a large smile. He opened the cell doors, removed the handcuffs from our wrists and began to speak.

'My friends, I've got good news for you,' his voice bounced. 'Your papers and tickets are ready. You're going home!'

Yanke, Texan, Kofi and Matthew jumped with joy. Happiness was written all over their faces and their eyes glinted with hope. When they looked at me, I smiled. It hadn't quite sunk in for me and I didn't want to hamper everyone's newly found hope. Home. It was better than where I was now, but what would I be going back to? Although the thought of leaving the Gabonese Gendarmerie deserved a smile, it demanded nothing more.

The rest of the night continued with the usual entertainment François offered but this time, instead of our weary bodies dancing away into the night, we danced with a renewed hope — a hope that I sadly did not share.

'François!' a gendarme shouted. 'The commandant's car is about to arrive.'

François quickly gave us some fruit and then spoke to us.

'I will not be coming to work tomorrow.'

His words struck me.

'My shift patterns have changed,' François continued. 'I will start working day shifts and I'll only work weekends. But don't worry! You will be deported soon.'

There was a long pause.

'Take care of yourselves my friends. I will try to see to it that you are treated fairly. You have been wonderful detainees, and if any one of you is thinking of escaping, you will not go very far before they catch you.'

We all laughed.

He shook our hands and before we knew it, we had been locked into our cells again. We watched as François walked off into the distance. We only hoped that this would not be the last time we would see him.

In the days that followed, the gendarmes began to treat us well. Although we were handcuffed when we were taken out of the cell, they were taken off while we were in the cell. The situation had improved a little, but impatience would soon drive our thoughts insane and following a chain of thought became impossible. Since François' intervention, we had been given back some of our clothes, but we were still half-naked; the top half of our bodies remained bare and struggled to cope with the draught that constantly entered our cell. We couldn't wait to leave the cell. The only word that kept repeatedly reverberating in our minds was: home. When would we be going home?

It had been a week since François' departure and we still hadn't seen him. Exhaustion now weighed heavily on our bodies, even more so since we had last seen François. It was approaching 9am and in the distance, the figure of the commandant drew closer. He soon approached our cell.

'You will be deported back to your countries in two days,' he slowly relayed. 'You will be on transit to Libreville.'

After he had informed us of the procedures, he left us in an indifferent mood. Although our travels would now take us to the capital city of Gabon, our dream to get to Europe was now truly over. After all we had gone through we were now going back to the beginning. It was like painting a masterpiece, a work of art never dared before, and a man rises, lifts his hands and smears the canvas with black paint, damaging the kaleidoscope of colour. We were going back home, and it seemed like there was no way out.

We were to be accompanied by two gendarmes who would escort us to Libreville International Airport where we would board our flights back home. The procedure was simple: get to the airport, board the plane and go back home. To the Gabonese gendarmes, it was as simple as that.

The day of our departure soon came. We had all woken up early, anticipating the arrival of the Gabonese gendarmes. It seemed like our good friend would not return, but there were more important matters to face. Minutes went by slowly as we constantly glanced to each other, reassuring ourselves that today was the day we would be on our way out of Port-Gentil.

A group of gendarmes loomed in the distance. As the group began to draw nearer, the figure at the helm began to mimic the walk of someone we had come to love with each step and as he finally approached our cell, his protruding warm smile resonated. François had returned. Happiness walked across our faces and an impulsive gush of emotions took hold of us. As he opened our cells, he began to speak.

'My friends, I am happy to see you all.'

He provided us with clothes to cover our bodies, and sandwiches as well. Even though we were hungry, it was impossible to eat. What would happen within the next three hours was all the food we needed. When we made it to Libreville, we would board our flights home. François and a different officer were selected to accompany us till our final flights back home, while another three in addition to François and his counterpart would escort us to Port-Gentil Airport. Once we had donned our clothes, we were handcuffed again and escorted into the small vehicle that would transport us to the Port-Gentil Airport.

'You will be handcuffed until you enter the plane,' he explained. 'But after that, you will become free men.'

After spending almost a month in Gabonese detention, to be relieved of our predicament sounded ridiculous. In pain, anguish, and torment we waited to hear the words François spoke on the Wednesday I will never forget. We took beatings, groaned in pain, cried in anger, saturated the cold, stood for hours, wailed in hunger and suffered mental fatigue. How could I ever allow myself to forget the treatment? What did it mean to be a free man? Was François really telling us the truth? I gave way to tears.

We soon arrived at the local airport; a small, rectangular building. We were asked to exit the vehicle. Our clothes were dirty and we had not had a shower for almost a month. People began to stare at us; the humiliation was insufferable. I could not continue to raise my head, so I looked down, blocking the cynical judgments of people as I passed by. We were taken through the rear doors of the airport and then followed into the plane by François and another gendarme, while the other three left.

For the first time in my life, I boarded a plane and it felt good.

Chapter 2: Letting Migrants Free

After a few comfortable hours on the plane, we arrived at Libreville International Airport. We were taken through the arrivals tunnel and then to the immigration office. There was no talking, except between François and the airport officials. François and his colleague had to be seen as doing their job; he exchanged no eye contact with us. It was a different side to him, one that expected respect and disregarded fear; his authoritative stance even more prominent than before.

When our paperwork was finalised, François and his colleague escorted us into our final plane heading to Murtala Muhammed International Airport, Lagos. Once we boarded the plane, François removed the handcuffs from our wrists and sat us down. For the first time since we arrived, he smiled. But this smile was different; it was the smile that meant it was time to depart. He looked into our faces and spoke slowly.

'I wish I could help…'

His voice trailed as his emotions began to tear into his last few words. A single tear rolled down his cheek. He quickly wiped his face with his hands, so for us not to see. But we had seen it. He saluted to us like a military solider in front of his general, and once more beamed his smile.

'Adieu mes amis. C'était un plaisir.'

'Goodbye François,' we all replied. 'Adieu.'

François walked away with his colleague and out of the plane. That was the last time I ever saw François. Fifteen minutes later, an airhostess approached us. She stated that one of our deportation papers was missing. We explained that we were never in possession of the papers. On hearing this, she hurried out of the plane in search of François, but she couldn't find him. Minutes passed since the incident, and the plane had yet not begun to move. People started to become disgruntled, hurling insults at the airline. Suddenly, the airhostess returned with the airport manager and two Gabonese immigration officers and we wondered what was going on.

'I'm sorry but you will not be flying with us today,' the airport manager said. 'Some of your papers are missing. You will have to wait for the next available flight.'

Yanke intervened.

'Are you people serious? What do you mean?'

'Your papers are missing. We cannot let you fly.'

'This is a joke.'

Yanke looked around; none of us could speak. It seemed that there was no way the airport manager would let us fly. 'When is the next flight?'

'Next Wednesday,' the airport manager replied.

We gasped, but with nothing to do to help our situation, we were escorted out of the plane. We either cooperated, or we faced the full force; the plane was in a hurry. We left the plane, and watched as it flew high into the sky. We all bowed our heads.

'That could have been us,' I thought. 'That could have been us.'

We were taken into the immigration office where the airport manager left the immigration officers with us. A series of telephone calls were made. Apparently, the documents needed by the immigration office should have been handed over by François and, according to the Port-Gentil gendarmerie, they were. But they never turned up in the hands of the immigration officers. Further to this, it would take two weeks before our deportation papers would be ready again. The problem was that the gendarmes of the Port-Gentil gendarmerie had already completed the handover to the airport immigration officers. They bitterly complained, but resolved to enquire of their next course of action from their manager.

The immigration officers were friendly and both of them could speak good English. Jokes began to flow and it was easy to talk to them. We didn't feel like we were criminals or being detained; we felt normal. How hard that had been for so long. As evening approached, one of the officers began to surprise us.

'When the manager comes back, this could be your one-way ticket to freedom.'

What did they possibly mean? Would that mean we would be going back to Nigeria quicker than we had imagined?

'Consider yourselves free,' the officers repeated.

There was no way that was possible. It would take two weeks before all our papers would be ready. Kofi spoke in astonishment.

'Did you guys just hear that?'

The officers laughed. Not because of what Kofi had said, but how he had said it. Later that evening, the manager arrived. He came into the office and soon began asking questions about our journey, how we had been treated and how we had managed to end up with them. After hearing our story, he was disappointed with the treatment we had received. He was a friendly man; slow to speak and quick to listen. It was getting late, and all of us looked starved.

'All of you must be very hungry now,' he said.

He left us, and returned a few minutes later.

'Take this, and from now on, consider yourselves free.'

Into our hands he placed 1,000 CFA Francs each. This was surreal. What was the airport manager doing?

'Buy some food with the money,' the manager continued. 'And be free!'

'Thank you sir,' Yanke responded, almost bewildered.

We made our way outside the airport doors. It seemed weird. There was 1,000 CFA Francs in our hands and we didn't know what to do. We weren't sure what the manager meant. Did he mean we were free to buy food or free to enter Gabon? We began to think the latter was not possible. We searched outside the airport and could not see a shop open nearby; it was quite late. We went back inside the airport and bought some food. After we had finished eating, we began to make our way outside to get some fresh air. We were all thanking the immigration officers for not restricting us in any way. A few seconds before reaching the main airport doors, Kofi spoke.

'Guys, we are being senseless.'

'If you are senseless, I'm not!' Yanke replied.

We all laughed.

'Come on guys. Think about it,' Kofi continued. 'One of the officers told us earlier that when the manager comes it could be our freedom ticket. And then the manager tells us to consider ourselves free. Guys, this could be our opportunity.'

Matthew spoke.

'I think Kofi could be right, Yanke.'

'Wake up guys. You are sleeping,' Kofi urged.

An argument erupted. We became agitated and began arguing about an issue which should have had a straightforward answer. But the ambiguity left us in disarray. As we continued arguing, the airport immigration manager approached us.

'Bonsoir.'

'Bonsoir,' we replied.

'It is good to be free, eh?'

At once, Kofi began to run. We all ran after him, because at last we all knew he was right. The manager's words were the only piece of clarity we needed. We all jumped into a taxi.

'Où allez-vous?' the taxi driver asked.

We did not know what this meant. Texan, who had been picking up a bit of French replied.

'Nous ne comprenons pas Français. Seulement Anglais.'

'Ah d'accord. You going to the city motor park?'

To my great surprise, and in one voice, we all replied:

'Yes! Yes!'

We were free. It was almost impossible to believe that we were now in a Gabonese taxi, driving into the city and undergoing a new journey in our lives. Being free did not feel good — it felt awesome. While we were in the taxi, it proved fortunate that the taxi driver was Ghanaian; he was from the same country as Yanke, Kofi, Matthew and Texan. Kofi then opened up to him.

'Listen,' Kofi said. 'We have nowhere to go and we don't know anyone here. Please help us.'

Upon hearing the tone of Kofi's voice, the taxi driver implored himself to find out about our situation. We all introduced ourselves and stated our names, before Yanke explained how we arrived in Gabon. It seemed everywhere we went we would have to explain how we got there. Once Yanke had finished, the taxi driver spoke.

'Guys, I'm not taking you to city motor park,' he announced. 'We're heading to my place.'

I was shocked and grateful at the same time. Shocked because this man's gesture was extraordinary; not many people would meet five strangers on the road and be prepared to take them to their homes, so for him to do this perhaps illustrated his kind heart. But I was grateful because we would have a place to rest our head; in our condition, that was certainly important. Somehow we had escaped leaving Gabon. What would happen now? As we drove around Libreville that thought constantly went through my mind.

We reached the taxi driver's home at around 11pm. His home was rather small and could not accommodate all five of us so he then took us to his friend's home, a thirty minute drive away. We were warmly received by his friend, and allowed to stay there until the following morning. Of course, we were all anxious; perhaps we had made the wrong decision. Perhaps we would be caught by the Gabonese gendarmes, and did we really interpret what the airport manager meant correctly? Although speech came to us slowly, I believe that's what we all must have been thinking. The following day came, and we all woke early. The taxi driver arrived and explained his situation to us.

'I can only take two people,' the taxi driver told us. 'My home is not big enough for any more. So you must decide amongst yourselves who'll join me in my home.'

The taxi driver left the room to allow us to make a decision. After much deliberation, we finally agreed that Yanke, Kofi and Matthew had to leave. That would mean that Texan and I would be staying with the taxi driver. It was a hard decision to make. We had been together for so long, we had gone through everything together and now it was time for us to say goodbye. I felt like crying, and the others could see it. Kofi noticed first.

'C'mon, don't cry, we'll be back.'

They promised to visit us as soon as they could, but I couldn't hold back. The pain was too hard to bear. From boarding the ship in

Lagos, to our trials in the gendarmerie, we had given each other strength, held each other up when we were falling and truly become a family. It was a shame that we couldn't stay together, but that was how we split up.

The taxi driver's name was Evans. He was a friendly man who lived alone and loved to have us around. To allow us to forget our loss, he offered to take us around Gabon's capital, to which we agreed. Libreville was a beautiful city. With only about 300,000 people in its capital, it was much smaller than Lagos. The city had a lot of timber trees, and we could see large trailers transporting them from the forests and taking them to the port. It was a great trip, and allowed me to soak in everything that had happened within only a few days.

Our first week with Evans was entertaining. He made us feel welcome and we had a great time. I soon began settling into the Gabonese way of life. One day, in the second week of our stay, a problem arose. We were informed that we could not walk freely on the streets of Gabon without a *Carte de Séjour* or a resident permit. Gabonese gendarmes would begin stopping vehicles in the streets, on the motorways and begin to visit people's homes. If you were found without a permit, you would be deported or thrown into prison. Perhaps, if they were being nice, you would get a fine and they would let you go. But if you didn't have a permit, you had to be careful about where you went and for how long. We were warned that we had to be vigilant. But before Evans left the room, he muttered something that ignited a little fear in my heart.

'They will be caught,' he paused. 'At least once.'

He thought we didn't hear him we realised as Texan and I looked at each other.

It was difficult to survive in Gabon without a job, and finding a job was a problem on its own. You needed a permit to get a job. By profession, Texan was a painter. We were both hoping that he could find a painting job soon, so that we could get a little money. We worried for Yanke, Kofi and Matthew, especially since they had not come to visit.

My first few weeks in Gabon were tough.

Chapter 3: A Close Call

It had now been over a month since we arrived at Evans' home and money was hard to find. I was in desperate need of a job, but the fact that I could only speak English did not help my cause. I used gestures to express myself to people, anything to try and persuade anyone to give me a job. After travelling from place to place, I soon became frustrated at the fact that no person could understand what I was saying. All my attempts were futile and if life in the first few weeks was tough, it was now getting tougher. There was nothing I could do other than become a beggar.

Most mornings I would wake up early and take my position at a market close to where we lived. I would sit there, with a small cup on the floor, beseeching those who passed by for their spare change. I found out what spare change was in French, and as people passed I would say: *petite monnaie.* My situation became desperate. Although I was ashamed to beg on the streets, I had to survive. I had to eat. At times Texan joined me begging on the streets, but the shame became too unbearable for him so he looked for alternative ways to acquire food and money. It was a hard period, but my past experiences taught me that there will be tough days in life. I made a small amount of money from begging which kept Texan and I going. I was always appreciative to those who gave me food and money, constantly thanking them for their kind heart. Before I was given money, people would shake their heads and pity my condition. But what could I do? I only had two options: beg or steal. The latter never went through my mind.

I always thought about Mary, my aunt, during this time; about everything that she went through for my sake and how she willed me to achieve my dreams. It was upsetting to think that I wasn't able to repay her, and I tried very hard to put everything behind me. But she must have been extremely worried; both Mary and Joy, my sister, must have thought I was dead. I had been unable to contact them and if they both saw me, I know how devastated they would be. I began thinking about sending Mary a letter. All I had to do was raise some money for postage. But then I would think: would it be better for me to be dead to her or allow her to go through the pain of wondering when I would come back? Did it matter if I was alive? I couldn't help myself, let alone go back home and help Mary and Joy. What would Mary say if she found out that I had stowed away on a ship and now my current occupation was a beggar?

Still, despite these thoughts, life continued. It was a warm evening, and I hadn't made anything from begging that day. I was starving and in desperate need for food. As I started walking around the market, I noticed a woman at a stall. She sold cooked rice, stew, and beans as well as fried plantain. It was very similar to Nigerian food. I decided to approach her, hoping she would pity me. When I got to her stall, it was incredibly busy. The majority of her customers were marketers, with some taxi and bus drivers amongst them. I was very hungry, but apprehensive. I had no money to buy food, so I waited until late at night for people to leave. I hoped to beg for the food that she had left or she was waiting to throw into the garbage. When I saw everyone had left, I went to her.

'Please, I'm hungry and I need a job.'

'Sorry, I have no job,' the woman replied.

'I can wash,' I hurriedly responded. 'I can wash plates really well and very fast. I can show you.'

'What is wrong with you? I just told you, I have no job for you!' she shouted at me.

I began to beg her fervently. I even asked for food as payment for my job.

'You are a beggar; leave me alone, before I call the gendarmes.'

Her heavy handed response caused me to break into tears. 'Please ma, I don't need money. I'll work for food. Help me please, I'm hungry.'

The woman was moved with pity.

'It's okay, are you hungry?'

'I'm very hungry ma, very hungry,' I replied in a rush.

It was as if she felt my pain, and she was truly convinced that I was hungry.

'Okay,' she said. 'I will give you some food. You can also come back tomorrow.'

I fell onto my knees and began to thank her. She pulled me up quickly.

'It's okay. Come back tomorrow.'

She provided me with a meal and then gave me some food to take home. I ate until I was satisfied. With a wide smile, I left her stall and started going home. When I got home, I found Texan fast asleep, but the smell of food in my hand woke him up instantly. I gave him some to eat, and we saved some for the following day.

The next morning I continued my begging as usual, but today it was different. I knew a meal awaited me. The woman only arrived in the evening so I earnestly counted the hours until she arrived. As soon as evening came, I quickly made my way to the market. She was glad to see me and gave me the job I had asked for. I would now wash plates in return for food. I later found out that she was Beninese and that her name was Mama Senume; I called her Mama Maisey. When the night was over, she once again gave me some food to eat and to take home. I finally had a job. Although it didn't provide money, it gave me a lifeline. I could survive and to survive was the most important thing. I had never washed plates for a market seller before so it was a different experience, but I wasn't ashamed. Begging on the streets had almost made me invincible to the mocking judgments and unnecessary insults.

One day while I was at the stall washing plates a man came over to me and gave me 500 CFA Francs. I thanked him, but couldn't explain why he did it. It had been a while since I'd had money in my hands, but I decided that I had enough for postage; it had been over eight months since I'd left Nigeria and I knew they must be worried. As soon as I got home, I wrote a letter to Mary and Joy with the help of Texan and Evans. As I wrote, a tremendous smile began to grow on my face.

Dear Mary and Joy,

I know you would have been worried about me. But it must please you and me that I am alive. I was heading to Europe with a ship, but unfortunately I was unable to make it. I am in Gabon now. It is a French-speaking country and so it is hard for me to understand what they say. It is also compulsory for you to have a resident permit in order to stay in the country. I hope to get mine soon. Right now, I am well away from getting back to school because of the French. Nonetheless, I hope to get back to school soon. Don't worry about me. I am alive and healthy.

Speak to you soon.

I posted the letter the next day and hoped that I would receive a reply soon. The same evening, I went to Mama Maisey's stall, but she was nowhere to be found.

'She didn't tell me she wouldn't be in today,' I thought.

I waited for hours, hoping she would come. I hadn't eaten anything for the whole day. It was now approaching 11pm and I decided to return home. Fortunately, Texan had bought some food. I began to fear the worst. Was she really gone? Perhaps she was ill.

The next day, I went to the stall, but again she wasn't there. I didn't know where she lived, so it was impossible for me to see her. Mama Maisey was the only reliable source of food Texan and I had. Although Texan and I were looking for jobs, it wasn't easy to find a job without a permit and we still hadn't heard from Yanke, Kofi and Matthew. The hunger that had returned was hard for us to bear, and only sleep would make us forget. The day after, at sunrise, I went begging again while Texan went in search of a job. Although it was a positive move by Texan, nothing was going to happen soon. We both needed a permit; our situation was helpless. Who would give us a job?

While I was begging for money, a freshly polished taxi, almost as bright as the sun, pulled up close to where I was. The driver lowered his window and began asking me questions.

'Parlez-vous Français?'

'Non, seul petit. Anglais seul,' I replied.

'You speak English?'

'Yes sir.'

'I always see you on this road begging…' he paused. 'Why? What are you doing here?'

'Sir, I beg to survive,' I replied.

'What do you mean? Beg to survive?'

'I don't want to beg, sir,' I began to reveal. 'I beg for money to buy food and if people do not give me money, I beg for food. I do not wish to beg sir, but I need to survive.'

'You beg to survive?' he repeated. 'But for how long will you be doing this?'

'I don't know sir…I don't know.'

Upon hearing my response, he immediately introduced himself as Raufu. His nickname was *Eko* meaning Lagos. Eko was a man of average height, and slight body. His face was dark, but his yellow eyes made his wide nose even more prominent. He had surprisingly thin lips and I could tell that his hair was freshly cut by the sharp indents in his hair. Although he had a strong smile and was not a big man, his calm persona presented a sense of strength and understanding about him. He asked where I originated from, and I was surprised when he said that he was also from Nigeria. Eko and I talked for a while and before driving off he gave me 5,000 CFA Francs.

'Take this, and don't come here begging again.'

At first, I thought he was warning me, and was about to ask why, before he continued.

'I normally drive around these roads between 10am and 11am. Come to this same place. I will give you some money and try to look for a carwash job for you.'

Was this to be a change in my situation? Eko was showing an interest in me and I was glad. Later that day, I went to the market to see if Mama Maisey had returned. She hadn't; I hoped all was well as I could only wait to see if she came back to the market. I returned home to Texan and told him about Eko. We were both happy and hoped he would keep his promise.

'We just have to find a way out of our current situation,' said Texan.

The next morning I followed Eko's instruction. I left my home around quarter to ten in order to make my way to the market. As I turned left onto the main street, I saw three gendarmes and a group of people seated on the floor. My mind triggered back to the resident permit and I was immediately struck with fear. I didn't know whether to turn back or continue with my journey. I decided to turn back. As I began to do so, I was tapped on my back.

'Bonjour monsieur,' he said. 'Puis-je voir votre carte de séjour?'

I was confused. I didn't know what he was saying.

'Yes, yes,' I hurriedly answered.

Upon hearing my reply, the gendarme signalled to his colleague.

'Un Anglais.'

The gendarme's colleague approached me. 'Can I see your resident permit?'

My heart stopped. Evans had warned us, and now I was in the position we had tried so carefully to avoid. As the second gendarme approached me, I had already begun making my mind up that I would be deported. This time there was no way out. My silence was everything the gendarme needed to sit me with the rest of those they had caught. One of the people sitting down spoke to me.

'I was told that if you are stopped on the road,' he said solemnly. 'Without a resident permit by a gendarme, you will be put in prison and then deported.'

This man confirmed to me what Evans had said. To say that I was scared was an understatement. I remained quiet saying nothing. For over an hour, people were being dragged to the floor. Some cried while some tried to fight; others had a look on their face which showed that it was over. The gendarmes were cracking down and they were showing no mercy. Those who resisted were shown brute force. I began praying, hopeful that perhaps a force above would look down on me and help me out in my plight, hopeful that a miracle could happen. But another hour passed and nothing happened. By now, I had missed my appointment with Eko; everything was gone. As soon as I began to drift into my thoughts, a gendarme van swerved into the side of the road. The gendarmes guarding us began shouting quickly.

'Aller! Aller! Aller!'

We all stood up and the gendarmes began choosing who was to be put in the van. I was the first person selected. They got ten of us into the van and then drove off. There was a cold, menacing silence in the vehicle and it almost felt like we were being driven to our execution. After having driven for about an hour, we were pulled out of the vehicle. We all began to fear the worst as we saw cutlasses in the hands of the gendarmes. They arranged us all in a single line and began to take us deep into a field. All of us were frightened, not knowing what was happening and where we were going. The gendarme leading the line stopped and turned.

'Arrêter! Stop! Put out your hands.'

The five other gendarmes began to shout together.

'Put out your hands.'

'Mettre vos mains.'

We did as we were instructed. But the nervousness we had could be sensed. I was first in the line. Only one thought began to go through my head. What would happen to Mary and Joy? The gendarme raised the cutlass into the air — I closed my eyes — and brought the handle down to the palm of my hand. I breathed relief. The gendarmes began handing out cutlasses to the rest of the group.

'Take, take,' they said.

Each of us was given a portion of land and told to cut the grass with the cutlasses. One of the gendarmes came over to me.

'My name is André,' he said. 'Most of the people here will be deported, but some will be left free. Make sure you have your permit next time.'

Before I was able to thank him, he had walked away. Was André trying to tell me that I was being let go? The glimmer of hope I had begun to glow a little brighter. Once we had all finished, we were all put back into the van. The van drove for about twenty minutes, before it suddenly stopped.

'You, you, you. Get out.'

I was the first person picked again. I couldn't believe it; the gendarmes were letting me free. We got out of the vehicle quickly, and in an instant it drove off into the distance. I didn't know where I was; I was practically in the middle of nowhere. How would I get back home? One of the people who had been released knew the way back to the centre of Libreville and so we started walking. Once we had gotten to the city centre, I left him. I got home very late that night, losing my way a few times and asking for directions from people as I went along. As I narrated the events of the day to Texan, he was startled, but relieved to see me again. I began to reflect on my day as Texan left me to go and shower. Sadly, I had missed Eko's appointment and I hadn't had a chance to go to the market and see whether Mama Maisey was back. Although it was very late, I was determined to look for any signs as to whether she had come back and set off to the market. Unfortunately, she still wasn't there. Slowly, with my shoulders wilted, I made my way back home.

All in all, it had been a dreadful day. As I went to sit, Texan saw how sad I was.

'I have a surprise for you.'

'Please be quick,' I begged. 'I have no energy.'

From within the room, he brought out some food. By the smell, I could tell that it was smoked fish and rice. At once, I became agitated; fish and rice were expensive!

'Where did you get the money from?' I queried.

'I got two painting jobs today, so I bought some food.'

'Why didn't you tell me before I left?'

'I didn't know you were going to leave,' Texan responded. 'Moreover, I wanted you to rest a little.'

'This is good news, Texan,' I wearily answered. 'Please, let me eat.'

At once, sensing my fatigue, he gave me some food. It was a delicious meal and I was silent, enjoying and savouring every bite. Texan treated me and, although he couldn't see it now, I greatly appreciated his effort. He also gave me some money. Perhaps the day wasn't too bad after all.

The next morning, Evans came to speak to us and he didn't seem too happy.

'When are you leaving?' he asked, bluntly.

'What happened?' Texan replied.

'Nothing; it's just that you guys have overstayed.'

'Please give us some more time sir,' Texan pleaded. 'We are trying to find work. We'll leave soon, sir.'

Texan's plea worked; although Evans didn't look comfortable about it, he gave us more time, but it wasn't likely to be enough. Evans was a heavy smoker and drinker, and would always bring women home from the parties that he went to. Sometimes, when we were sleeping, he would wake us up and send us out of the house to wait until he called us back inside. For a period of time, Evans made our stay miserable, almost signalling for us to leave. We would have gone, but we had nowhere to go. We appreciated Evans' hospitality and kindness for letting us stay at his home, but we knew his generosity was running out.

Once Evans had left, I quickly made my way to the market, hopeful to see Eko. He said he saw me on this road every day, and perhaps he would see me again. This time, I was very careful, so as not be caught by a gendarme again. I waited in the market for several hours, but didn't see him. As I was about to leave, I saw Eko's taxi pull up beside me. He shouted over the great volume of the market.

'Why didn't you turn up yesterday?'

I explained what had happened yesterday and the events of this morning; he was extremely sorry for me. He asked me to sit in the front passenger seat of his car. We drove for three hours, whilst Eko picked up passengers in his taxi. We toured all of Libreville, and it was an enjoyable experience. Eko and I spoke a lot and we got to know each other better. He bought me some food, before dropping me at the place where he met me. He was determined to help; at least, that's what I believed. He asked me to come to the same place the following day.

The next morning, I saw Eko again. Before, I could greet him, he spoke hurriedly.

'I've just come to pick you up. Remember that carwash job I spoke about?'

'Yes?'

'Good news! There's an opening!'

Eko informed me that the owner of the carwash, Rocky, had come back from holiday and that he had told him of my experience.

'The man wants to see you!' He ecstatically told me.

I cried, though I don't remember why. Perhaps it was mental exhaustion; the culmination of the incidents over the past few days, or just pure happiness, but I cried. It was a weird feeling; Eko hugged me. When I arrived at Rocky's home, he wanted me to start immediately. But he soon realised it wasn't possible because of how physically weak I looked. I was then told to start work at 9am and finish at 7pm, every Monday to Saturday. Although I only received 1,000 CFA Francs a day, it was more than I made on the streets.

The first day of my carwash job was stressful, but I enjoyed it. Only a few days ago it had felt like there was no purpose in my life. Now I had some sort of direction; there was some sort of plan.

Chapter 4: Moving Out

It had been a while since I'd sent a letter to Mary and Joy, and I wasn't sure whether they had received my first one yet. Perhaps they thought I was dead by now. What hope would they have? As I constantly revisited these thoughts, singing became a way to console myself. I sang while walking in the streets, while eating, in fact I sang whenever I could. Some people would look at me, and give me that puzzled look, which suggested I was insane, but I didn't care. What did it matter?

I had been in the carwash job for about two weeks now and everything was going well. While working one day, Rocky's young son approached me and asked me a question that surprised me.

'Why aren't you in school?'

I began to think of a response, and all my past memories seemed to whirl past me. The pause was long and his young eyes beckoned a response, but I couldn't answer. Rocky's son was eight years old and the inquisitiveness in his stare was all too easy to recognise. I knew he wouldn't leave me alone until I gave an answer to his question.

'School…I will go to school. I know I will.'

The disappointment of my answer was written bold on his face.

'When will you go back to school?' he asked.

'Soon.'

The question struck me so hard it felt like I had been dealt a blow to my cheekbone. My gritty determination not to cry caused teardrops to build in my eyes; I quickly walked away from the boy.

The irony of it all was that my problems all began at eight. I could no longer withhold my tears and I swiftly made my way to the gents' toilet, and wept loudly. While in the toilet, I was called to attend to a customer. My swollen eyes were easily noticeable, and so I splashed water on my face. As soon as I made my way towards the customer's vehicle, my eyes were noticed. I quickly attempted to swivel my head away from the customer's direction, but they had caught sight of me.

'Why are you crying?' the customer asked.

I couldn't speak. I didn't think I wanted to cry as much as I did, but I couldn't control myself. In my mind, I would like to have stopped, but the emotional weight on my shoulders was heavy and my body felt it was time to let go. Every time I tried to talk, tears would flow. The customer soon saw that I was inconsolable and walked away. I stopped trying to talk and tried to get on with my job. For the whole day, I would reflect on the words of Rocky's son; it was a reminder of where I was coming from. Although the whole day had been woefully upsetting, it made me appreciate where I was. I was somewhat safe, with a job and surviving. Survival was always important.

Two months after the incident, while I was washing a car, I noticed another car pull in. As usual, I would hand over the car to my colleague and move on to the next car and get the process of washing started. As the windows of the car lowered, I was reunited with a man from my past. It was the airport immigration manager who had given Yanke, the others and I 5,000 CFA Francs at the airport. I hesitated before I approached his car. I started thinking about what to do, what to say. What would he think? Here I was, in Libreville without a permit. The man had probably let us go with the predisposition that he would never see us again. But here he was. Here I was!

'What if I just departed on a break for a few minutes then re-appeared when he had finished?' I thought.

As soon as I was to take a decision, he called out.

'Peter, Peter,' he beckoned me. 'Come and wash my car. Come, come.'

How did he remember my name? It had been months since we had last met, and judging by his attitude, it seemed like he hadn't recognised me yet. He acted like he'd never met me before. I was somewhat surprised. But he knew my name.

'Peter, Peter,' another customer shouted, as they pulled in.

It then occurred to me that my colleagues were shouting my name and thus customers were trying to vie for my attention, in order for me to wash their cars first. My racing heart began to settle. I went to the airport manager's car and gave it one of the best washes I had ever done. When I was done, I gave him back his key and collected the fee.

'Thank you Peter,' he said. 'The car is very clean.'

He placed the money into my hands, closed my fingers into the palm of my hands, winked and walked away. I counted the sum in my hands and realised he had given me a tip. Funnily enough, it was 1,000 CFA Francs. Perhaps, he did remember me. But since then I was a little uncomfortable with working at Rocky's place.

A few weeks later, it occurred to me that it had been a long time since I'd been to the market to see if Mama Maisey was back. I decided that I would go the next day and when I arrived, I saw another woman selling food at her stall. I approached her and asked if she knew where Mama Maisey was. I was told she was ill. I was terribly upset, and decided the least I could do was to pay her a visit. I asked whether she had Mama Maisey's address and if it would be okay for me to visit her. She said I should come back the next day.

I went back the next day to see the woman and she gave me Mama Maisey's address. When I arrived at Mama Maisey's home, I met her husband Joseph, who was also known as Baba Senume. They were both happy to see me. I spent some time with them and assisted with some domestic duties.

'Mama Maisey,' I began to ask just as I was leaving. 'I was wondering whether I could still wash plates at the market for food?'

'No problem, Peter. Anytime you're ready.'

I left with a smile that would even make a Cheshire cat jealous.

Texan was still in search of a job, and life at Evans' home became more unbearable by the day. His hostility towards our stay became more revealing as the days went by and it was clear that he wanted us out as soon as possible. He would always say how he had only let us stay in his home for a maximum of two months, to get ourselves sorted, and now we had been in his place for over a year. Tension was building. But aside from the perennial harassment Evans relentlessly bestowed, we were concerned with the perpetual patrols of gendarmes in our municipality. One day, it was very early in the morning and Evans, Texan and I were fast asleep, when a neighbour began to belligerently hit the door.

'Contrôle! Contrôle!' The gendarmes had come.

As soon as Texan and I heard those words, we opened one of the windows at the back of Evans' home, and jumped through. We ran, hiding in the nearby vegetation, which was at least 5 feet tall. We laid low and watched how the gendarmes surrounded the vicinity. How they, without mercy, pulled families and individuals from their homes because they didn't have a permit. It was harrowing to watch. We looked at each other and our silence spoke for itself.

Our freedom was prohibited because of the *Carte de Séjour.* We couldn't freely visit anywhere we wanted, we couldn't get a job, and as a result money was hard to get. Later that evening, I went to see Mama Maisey and tell her about my situation. She was well again and back in the market. She promised to look for a room for me near where she lived. The only problem was that I had no job, which would make it extremely difficult for me to pay the rent. Fortunately, Mama Maisey needed someone to help her at home with domestic duties and so we both agreed that I would be paid in exchange for being the house help.

A few days later, Mama Maisey informed me that she had found me a place to stay. I was elated. It was a small room, and only big enough for one person.

At Mama Maisey's home, she explained to me my duties.

'You will be cutting timber trees,' she explained. 'And doing some small house jobs.'

For me, this was great news; I had another source of income and a place I could call home. I spoke to Texan about it and he was happy though there was sadness in his not being able to come with me. As I began to pack my clothes in readiness to leave Evans' home, I decided that it wouldn't be fair not to tell him where I was going. After all, Evans had been good to us. Although he spent most of his time with prostitutes, drinking and smoking, he had kept us both in his home for over a year, where many would have simply thrown us out. But he was the least of my priorities. The joy of leaving Evans' abode overwhelmed me.

As I began thinking about what to pack, what time I would leave and when I would tell Evans we were leaving, my mind touched upon a memory I allowed myself to forget — Yanke, Kofi and Matthew. For over a year, Texan and I had waited and still they didn't come. It hurt Texan and I that the men we had come to know as our friends did not return and that we didn't know where they were. If I left Evans' home, Texan would be left alone and the group would truly be separated. Perhaps the hardest fact for us to swallow was that Yanke, Kofi and Matthew could still be alive…or they could have been tortured until they could survive no longer. But no matter what the scenario, it proved to me that the stage of life we were going through was survival and living came second. That meant I had to go.

A week later, after Mama Maisey had arranged the terms of my new room, I decided to tell Evans I was leaving. There was no joy or elation in his face.

'Okay,' he said. 'Good luck.'

It was weird to say the least, but I decided not to dwell too long on his mood. Texan followed me to help me settle in; he wished we could stay together, but knew that it would be too difficult because of the size of the room. The area was called *Village de André*, which was near to *Village de Mama Cathy* in Lalala Adroit.

Every morning I would wake up at 5am and assemble the fresh wood in a pile, carefully place it on the stump of a fallen tree and use a sharp axe to split the wood. It was a hard task, but it gave me something to do. After I'd finish cutting the wood, I would then take it to Mama Maisey. She would use some as fuel to cook breakfast, and keep the rest for later. Later in the evening, I would follow Mama Maisey to the market stall, where we would sell the food being cooked, coming home at 9pm or 10pm at times. Although it was a stressful job, I always did it with a smile. I had something to keep me busy and I was earning money to take care of myself.

A few weeks later, late at night, I heard someone knocking on my door. With weary eyes, I looked up at the time: 11pm. I asked who it was, but the sound I heard was simply a mumble. I was too tired to listen properly.

'Peter, Peter,' the voice continued.

As I got closer to the door, the voice sounded familiar. I switched on the light and opened the door.

'Texan!' I shouted. 'What are you doing here at this time?'

'Quiet down, Peter,' he loudly whispered. 'I know. I know. I'll explain to you what's going on. Just let me in please.'

I quickly let Texan in. I was surprised to see him. In his hands, he was carrying his rucksack, which meant that this wasn't going to be a short term visit.

'Evans threw me out,' Texan explained. 'I told him I had nowhere to go, but he wouldn't listen.'

'Oh no...'

'I had nowhere to go Peter…I only had you.'

'I can't believe this,' I said. 'And he didn't tell you why he wanted you to leave?'

'He just said I should go. He said you had gone, so I had to too. I don't know where to go Peter. Please help me.'

You can imagine my dilemma: in a room where it was just about manageable for one person to live, I now had to share with Texan. What if Mama Maisey found out? What would she say? I didn't know what to do, but my friend was in dire need of help.

'Alright, alright. We'll think of something in the morning. Just get yourself sorted out.'

That night, like many other nights, I had a nightmare. This seemed to be a frequent occurrence now, and I hated it. Some nights I would dream about my past, how I slept in the abandoned building, and other nights I would dream about my future, whether I would survive. Texan always had to bear my screaming at nights, but I guess he had gotten used to it. Our situation was ugly to say the least, but Texan and I were battling through. I just wondered when the battling would end.

Chapter 5: My Third Mother

On my way to meet Mama Maisey, I met a middle-aged man sitting down on a bench. He was short and stocky, wore a yellow t-shirt that heavily contrasted his dark skin, and spoke with a warm voice. Although his name was Shadrach, people in the area called him Papa Juju. Papa Juju was a professional carpenter. He was also my neighbour although I'd never seen him until that day. I heard he had done a lot of painting jobs and decided to speak to him.

'Bonjour monsieur. Parlez-vous un peu l'anglais?'

'Bonjour young man. How can I help?'

'I'm your neighbour sir. It's nice to meet you.'

I shook his hand.

'It's nice to meet you too.'

'I heard you're a painter, sir?'

'Yeah, why d'you ask?'

'I was wondering if…I mean that my friend and I are looking for a job. So if you need any helpers, sir…'

He knew what I was trying to say instantly.

'At the moment, there are not many jobs out there. But I will speak to my director. What is your friend's name?'

'Texan, sir.'

'And you?'

'Peter.'

'Okay Peter, I will speak to my director about whether you and Texan can get a painting job,' he continued. 'You good at painting?'

I couldn't tell him that I didn't know how to paint; I quickly thought of an answer.

'My friend is better.'

'Well, we'll see soon. Won't we?'

'Yes sir. Thank you very much for giving us the opportunity.'

'No problem.'

'I'm on my way to somewhere now, but it was nice speaking to you.'

'See you soon then.'

A few weeks later, Papa Juju invited me to meet his Director. I didn't know what I would face, so the night before, I queried Texan on everything I needed to know about painting. The next day I followed Papu Juju to meet the Director. Before we left for the Director's office, Papu Juju spoke to me.

'You never *really* answered my question when we first met.'

I had no idea what Papa Juju was talking about.

'What was that?'

'Can you paint?'

My heart stopped.

'Me sir,' I said, pointing at myself, trying to buy myself some time.

'Yes.'

What would I say?

'Well, not really.'

Oh no, what had I said! Surely, I'd blown it.

'I thought so,' Papa Juju said. 'Bring your friend along.'

Relief overwhelmed me.

Papa Juju waited for me, while I went to get a delighted Texan to join me. Twenty minutes later, we both met up with Papa Juju again. He spoke to Texan and quickly realised that he was much more of a painter than I ever was. However, Papa Juju had already given my name to the Director as the main individual, while Texan was my assistant. Papa Juju got a bit worried that I may not be able to answer any technical questions that the Director might ask, but I told him that if he did, Texan had given me a tutorial the night before. All I had to do was enter the interview, answer a few questions, and get the job. I felt I was ready.

We soon arrived at the Director's office. We greeted the Director and took a seat. Papa Juju sat to my left, while Texan sat at my right. I introduced myself. To my surprise, the Director did not ask any technical questions. Instead, he simply told us where we were posted, what the task was and when we should start. We spent fifteen minutes in his office, and left soon afterwards. We were all delighted! Texan and I had a good job, and it gave a good wage too! This was marvellous news.

Two days after the interview, we visited the Director's office again. He took us to a site – in Carrefour Leon Mba in Libreville – and showed us where we would be painting. He showed us the paints we would be using and instructed us when he wanted the job completed. I had no clue about how to begin and Mr Charles, the Director, wanted us to begin while he was standing in the room. I was nervous. Texan and I wanted him to leave before we began work. Texan had only given me a theory-based introduction into painting, but now I had to have my first practical in the full glare of the Director. I decided to employ a well-known tactic: stalling. I began to explain to Texan what he had explained to me about painting like he was my apprentice. Soon after I began talking, Mr Charles left us. Relaxing as we were left, Texan began teaching me how to paint. He painted the complicated areas of the room, while I perfected my technique on the easier parts. I was happy with my teacher; he didn't rush me, but let me take my time. I would soon become his apprentice.

We had spent about three days painting the rooms in the building and, after Texan's practical lessons, I was soon painting with ease. A few more days passed, and Texan and I were both due to be paid. Because of *contrôle,* Mr Charles would usually give us a lift to work. Through our time so far, we had convinced Mr Charles that I was the main painter and Texan was my assistant or labourer. So when I approached him for our pay, he simply gave it to us. The money was quite large, and would sustain us until our next pay.

Although I worked with Texan, I was still able to help Mama Maisey chop the timber trees and carry out some domestic tasks. One day, Mama Maisey discovered that Texan was living me. I went into the house to drop the wood as I usually did every morning, when she spoke to me.

'Peter,' she said. 'Why didn't you tell me?'

'Tell you what, ma?'

'That you have decided to take in Texan.'

Oh no, I thought. She's found out and I've forgotten to tell her.

'I'm sorry ma. I didn't mean to.'

'For how long has he been staying with you?'

'For a couple weeks now.'

'Peter, Peter, Peter,' she repeated. 'How many times did I call your name?'

'Three times, ma.'

'So you're listening to me.'

'Yes ma.'

'Next time, please inform me when someone will be visiting you permanently for a couple of weeks. Okay?'

'Yes ma. It was just that Texan had nowhere to go and I forgot. I'm sorry ma. It won't happen again.'

'It's okay. Drop the wood over there.'

I thought Mama Maisey would be angry that I let in Texan, but she wasn't. She showed love and mercy towards Texan and I, and I was very grateful.

More days passed, and all of sudden, an air of stability seemed to surround my life. Nothing unusual or unpleasant had happened for the past few days, and I was enjoying my company with Texan. I was lying on my bed, back down, when my thoughts trailed to Mary. It had been a long time since I'd written a letter to Mary, and I didn't know whether she was alive and well. I knew it wasn't possible for her to send me a reply, because even if she did, I had no postal address. Though, I longed to read words from her. The next day, I spoke to Papa Juju about whether I could use his postal address to correspond with Mary. Papa Juju was glad to help. I quickly put pen to paper:

Dear Mary,

I know it has been two years since we last spoke and I am sorry that I did not give you a chance to contact me. I only realised soon after I'd sent you the letter that there was no way for you to reply. Things have been quite rough over these past two years, but I have moved to another place.

I met Mama Maisey at the market and she has been very helpful to me. She arranged a new place for me to live, and I am now a bit happier. I am working as a painter at the moment. My new friend Texan taught me how to paint. I started about a month ago, and I think I can now call myself a professional painter.

Hopefully, one day, I will get back to school and finish my education.

Please write me to this address BP: 1533, Libreville, Gabon.

I miss you mum. Please greet Joy for me.

Your son,

Peter.

It was late and I desperately desired to post the letter that night, but I had to wait. Finally, I could write to Mary and she could write me back. The very next day, while Texan and I were at work, I asked him if he could allow me to post the letter. I used a first class postage stamp, hoping that the letter would get to Mary as soon as possible.

We worked on the building in Carrefour Leon Mba for almost four months before we were transferred to work on another site. Texan and I were pleased with the change in our lives. Stability felt good. Finally, we didn't have to beg on the streets. We could earn our money, take care of ourselves and try to find a purpose to our lives. Was this the end of my predicament? Was this the better life I was in search for? Although I still knew that education was one of my major priorities, everything was moving at a steady pace. From day to day, I began planning how to get back into education, but it all seemed too difficult. Not only was I in a French-speaking country, how was I going to cope with teaching again? For now, it was a question I would leave unanswered.

A few months later, while I was coming back from work, I saw an elderly woman. She was short, slim and wore a yellow African headscarf around her head. She moved slowly across the floor, and her gaze presented one of innocence and serenity. Her face was quite light so that you could see her lips and eyes, which was quite unlike the sun-baked skin of the other African people I had encountered. She was carrying heavy goods in her basket, and was attempting to pick up another bag. She looked like she had too much to carry, and her farm produce kept on falling out of her basket, as she went to pick up the fallen food from the ground. I was walking in her direction and it looked like she needed help. But as I walked past her, I quickly grasped some of the bags before they slipped out of her hands. I helped her carry the goods home. When we reached her home, she asked me where I was living. After I told her where I lived, she gave me a banana that she had brought from the farm, but I refused to take it from her hands. She insisted, and so I gave in and took it, bidding her goodbye as I did. I ate the banana on my way back home and it was mouth-wateringly delicious. Perhaps helping her wasn't such a bad idea…

The following day, Texan and I were told that our contract would soon come to an end. No doubt, we would be jobless again. Texan and I had saved some money, but we didn't have a plan to sustain ourselves for a long period of time. Nonetheless, Mr Charles promised us that as soon as another site came up, he would call us straight away. We just had to be patient.

One Saturday morning, in the middle of 1987, it was just like any other day. Sunrise brought an explosion of colour to the world, and the birds' approval was easily heard. As I left my home, I noticed two women standing only a few metres away from my door. Ahead of me, was an average height African, perhaps Congolese judging by her face, plucking breadfruit from a tree. I didn't notice anything odd. As I walked past them, one of the women called my name.

'Mon enfant,' she continued. 'Bonjour. Vous rester ici?'

The voice sounded familiar, and as I turned around, I noticed that it was the elderly woman I had helped the other day.

'Oui, je reste ici.'

'D'accord. Quand nous avons rencontrés, je n'ai jamais dit mon nom. Mon nom est Mama Cathy et je vis dans le village suivant. Comment allez-vous mon enfant?'

'D'accord. My French is not so good… Mon français n'est pas très bon, mais je vais bien. Merci. Et vous?'

'Oui, je suis bien. Où allez-vous mon enfant?'

'Je vais travailler.'

'Ahh. Allez! Allez! Vous serez en retard. Mais un jour, vous devez venir à ma maison.'

I looked at my watch. She was right; I was going to be late.

'Je vais Mama Cathy! Merci. À bientôt!'

I waved goodbye.

On my way, I thought about Mama Cathy. She kept on calling me *mon enfant*, she could only speak a little English and she was very friendly. The woman who was standing beside her could speak good English. I also considered the invite that she had given me. There was a lot of food for thought as I continued to work.

A week later, I visited Mama Cathy as promised. I saw her with the woman that I had met the other day. They were cutting grass using cutlasses. Seeing what they were doing, and with a lot of spare time on my hand, I swiftly moved to action. We worked throughout the day and I was happy to be there.

'Couper l'herbe me maintient en forme.'

I nodded and smiled, not entirely sure what she was saying. Realising this, the woman beside her spoke.

'She said "Cutting the grass keeps me fit." Better?'

'Oui,' I replied.

From time to time, I would visit Mama Cathy's home and help her cut the grass. Although our communication was not free-flowing, there was a motherly love present and it was evident to see. One day, I went to Mama Cathy's home to cut grass and on my way home, I met Mama Maisey.

'Hello Peter, where are you coming from?'

'I'm coming from Mama Cathy's home.'

'Oh,' she said. 'That is the landlady of Village de Mama Cathy. What were you doing there?'

'I went to help her cut the grass around her home.'

'That's very nice that you helped her.'

I was told that Mama Cathy had no child of her own and her mother was mentally ill. It came as terrible news to me and I was deeply upset. Although I was only beginning to get to know Mama Cathy, she was such a nice woman and it didn't feel right that she had to go through that.

When I visited Mama Cathy's home, I saw a woman in her 80s. Her clothes were dirty and her face didn't move. She stared blankly. I greeted her, but she gave me no response. I asked Mama Cathy who the woman was, and whether she was okay. Mama Cathy told me that that was her mother. While I was talking to Mama Cathy, I heard someone calling my name. It sounded like Papa Juju.

'Peter! Peter!'

'What happened?'

'I've got a letter for you,' he shouted.

'What?!'

I ran towards Papa Juju and grabbed the letter with excitement. It was from Mary. I couldn't believe my eyes. I told Mama Cathy I had to go, and began running home. Mama Cathy tried to call me back.

'Your food! Your food! I've got food for you, and some money!'

I couldn't think about food or money. For over two years, I'd waited for this moment and I wanted to enjoy it. As soon as I arrived home, I shut the door behind me, opened the letter with an infinite amount of care and started reading.

My Dear Son Peter,

I am happy you are well! I am well too! Your sister is doing well and we have both been worried sick about you. And we received your first letter.

Joy has finished secondary school and has just enrolled on a nursing course. Things were never the same after you left. Tony is well, but no one has told him where you are.

Please remember your education and do your utmost to get back to school someday. There is so much to tell you and I hope one day, I will see you again.

Take care my son, and God bless you.

Your mum,

Mary.

It had been over two weeks now since I'd been to Mama Cathy's home. Meanwhile, Texan and I had no job. Mr Charles promised to call us when there was a vacancy, but we knew we couldn't wait on him. We thought it would be best if we began to look for a better life elsewhere. Although being a painter provided a good source of income, it was nothing permanent and that meant stability wouldn't be permanent as well. We both decided that Texan would make a move first.

Two weeks after our discussion, Texan left for another city. It was one of the most emotional days of my life. Texan and I were practically close enough to be called brothers. We had survived so much together. For more than two years now, we'd struggled through hardship and built our way into a country that we knew nothing about. We hustled for everything, supported each other in our hour of need and pushed each other when we had nothing left to give.

'Peter,' Texan said, with tears brimming in his eyes. 'I am going to miss you.'

'I am going to miss you too,' I cried.

I hugged Texan and we embraced for a long time. He promised to come back for me and hoped to have a better life where he was going. We both looked at each other. Texan spoke first.

'Make sure you take care of yourself Peter. I'll be back. You won't even notice if I've gone.'

'You too, Texan. If we don't meet again, just know it was a pleasure to have known you in my life.'

I burst into tears again. Texan pulled my head into his shoulder, and held my head.

'Don't worry, Peter,' he continued. 'Come on. Don't cry. It'll be okay. You need to have courage and strength now. Take heart.'

I tried to stop crying. I carried Texan's bags to the side of the road where the farm driver would pick him up. Between us, we had saved a small amount of money. I gave Texan some of it, but he refused to take it.

'I've already got some money for food. Don't worry.'

The farm driver's vehicle dropped into the side of the road, and we loaded Texan's bags into the boot. I watched Texan enter the car and waved one last goodbye. The vehicle drove off.

I didn't know where Texan was going. Perhaps that would be the last time I would ever set my eyes on him in my life. It was a truly touching moment. The morning Texan left, set the mood for the remainder of the day. I was by myself now. It was me against the world. My brother had gone.

A month passed since Texan had left and I was still jobless. I couldn't continue depending on Mama Maisey before I ate every day and it was hard to pay the rent, especially when I could only work for food. One morning, I got extremely frustrated and annoyed with myself. In haste, I took my clothes and a little money that I had with me and went to the bus garage, in search of the farm driver that had taken Texan away. I wanted to leave. I had heard rumours that Texan was now working in another village, and so perhaps life would be a little easier for me there. But before I went, I had to hand over the room key to Mama Maisey.

'Mama Maisey, Mama Maisey,' I called. 'I need to talk to you.'

'What's happened, Peter?'

'Nothing. I'm just handing over my room key.'

'Why? Have you found another place?'

'Not exactly... I'm travelling.'

'Travelling? To where?'

'I want to visit Texan.'

'Peter, Peter, Peter,' she repeated. 'How many times did I call your name?'

'Five times Mama. You cannot change my mind.'

'Peter,' she continued. 'Nobody knows where Texan is. All we are hearing is rumours and now you want to be gallivanting in search of him. Peter, rethink.'

'What is there to rethink? There is nothing left for me here. Nothing! I have work to put a single meal into my mouth. I can't do it anymore Mama Maisey. I can't do it anymore.'

I cried. Baba Senume spoke.

'You can't just wake up and say you are going to another city.'

'But I just can't keep coming to you and asking you for food.' I replied.

'But we're not complaining Peter. Are we?'

I gave him a look that suggested there was no hope. He looked at his wife and shook his head.

'I'm sorry, but I just can't wait any longer.'

'How much do you need?' Mama Maisey asked.

'I don't need anything, please.'

I quickly handed over the key. Although I tried to resist, Mama Maisey also gave me some money. I hugged them both and thanked them deeply for everything they had done for me. With my mind made up, I left; and though I insisted he didn't need to, Mama Maisey's husband escorted me to the road. As we got to Carrefour IAI, a major roundabout, we met another opposition.

'Bonjour mes enfants. Où allez-vous ce matin?'

Before I could respond, Baba Senume intervened.

'Il essaie de fuir tout le monde. Nous avons essayé de l'arrêter, mais il ne veulent pas entendre.'

I wasn't running away from everybody. I was just going to visit Texan.

'Quoi?'

Mama Cathy had called for me several times, but she said I was nowhere to be found. She wasn't happy with my change in behaviour.

'Mon enfant, vous êtes en fuite?'

Before I could reply, she clutched my bag, held my hand like I was a small child and dragged me. I was running behind her, while she was speed walking away from the side of the road. Baba Senume began laughing hysterically at how I looked. As soon as we reached Mama Cathy's home, she spoke.

'Here. Key. Take.'

What was she doing?

'La nourriture est dans la cuisine. Vous voulez un emploi? I will give job.'

She instructed me to stay in her home until she came back from the farm. I didn't think she was being serious. I was going; no one was going to stop me. But Baba Senume kept on laughing.

'You're not going anywhere.'

Soon after, Baba Senume left me alone in Mama Cathy's home. Her home was untidy, and so I decided to give it a clean. Later in the afternoon, while walking around Mama Cathy's home, I spotted a large, friendly dog. When I turned my head left, I saw Mama Cathy's mother, Ayito. I soon realised that the dog belonged to her. Ayito's room was dirty, smelled and was severely in need of a clean. It was packed with clutter. I was moved with pity, and tidied up around her. The dog stank like it was an ancient artefact that had been buried in a peat bog for almost a thousand years, so I bathed the dog as well. The rear of the building was pervasive with high-growing vegetation, clutter and mini-swamp puddles, so I decided to tackle that too. After I'd finished tidying up, my clothes were wet, muddy and smelled, but the job was done. Later that evening, Mama Cathy arrived home from the farm, walked around her home and went into Ayito's room. She stayed there for almost two hours. I was worried and wondered what was going on. I knocked on her door. As soon as I opened, Mama Cathy spoke.

'Je sais que vous avez nettoyé la chambre de Ayito. Thank you mon enfant.'

It was still hard to communicate with Mama Cathy as although I had stayed in Gabon for over two years, I had only learned certain phrases in French. But that night Mama Cathy really wanted to speak to me. She called for Mama Celine, the woman living next door, to translate for us. When I saw her, I soon realised that she was the woman who was always with Mama Cathy.

Mama Cathy insisted that she wanted to know everything about me. Mama Celine translated.

'You are a good boy. Everyone in the village says good things about you. I would like to know how you got here,' said Mama Cathy.

I didn't know where to begin or how to start. I was confused. It was difficult for me to explain to Mama Cathy all the terrible trials I went through. But she insisted that I tell her. She wanted to know who my mother was, who my father was and how I ended up in Gabon. As I was about to explain, I began crying. It was too emotional for me to relive the memories again. She sympathised with me.

'It's okay mon enfant. Ça va, ça va. It's okay.'

Mama Cathy became very upset that she had forced me to start talking. Mama Celine translated.

'We shall talk about it later.'

Chapter 6: 'It's good to be free'

Mama Cathy took me with her and showed me to a room opposite to Ayito's where I would be sleeping.

'Mon enfant, this is your room. You must be very tired now. Follow me to the kitchen. I will get you some food,' Mama Cathy said.

Mama Cathy repeatedly referred to me as *mon enfant*, and I was beginning to get a little agitated. I didn't know what it meant, and my name was certainly not *mon enfant*. I had told her that my name was Peter, but she didn't take notice. I sought advice from Mama Celine.

'Why does Mama Cathy keep calling me mon enfant? Please tell her my name is Peter.'

At this, Mama Celine began to laugh. I looked at her blankly.

'Why are you laughing?'

'Mon enfant means my child,' she continued laughing.

Mama Cathy noticed how much Mama Celine was laughing and asked what was happening. When Mama Cathy found out, she started laughing also.

'Englishman, please go bed.'

Although I was allowed to remember my depressing past, in the midst of it all, I still had something to laugh about.

A few days later, Mama Cathy sent for me and raised the same topic. She desired to know more about me. Mama Celine was present to help with translation.

'Mon enfant, I am deeply sorry about what happened the other day. I hope we can talk now.'

Although I felt much better, and a little more prepared, talking about my past was something I abhorred. I didn't like to dwell on my mistreatment, as it would only cause the heavy pain in my heart to bog me down. But Mama Cathy was different – she had helped me a lot. I composed myself and began to tell Mama Cathy my story from beginning to end.

'I was fifteen years old when I found out that the mother I once knew was never really my mother, but my dad's sister.'

'They hid the truth from you?'

'Yes. I was told by an old, drunk woman at a party in my village that my mother died when I was seven months old.'

Mama Cathy couldn't believe what she heard. She was devastated. Mama Celine was also shocked.

'What's your mum's and dad's name?' Mama Cathy asked.

'My biological mother's name is Elizabeth. My dad's name is Tony and his sister's name is Mary.'

Mama Cathy was shocked to hear how the events of my life had unfolded.

'Why did you leave Nigeria and come to Gabon?

I began to cry. I told her I ran away with a ship, and was later arrested by Gabonese gendarmes. I then narrated how we were miraculously freed, how I begged on the streets and all the events that led up to me meeting her. After I narrated the entire story, she couldn't hold back her tears.

'You've gone through all of this,' she said. 'But why did it have to be like this?'

Mama Cathy couldn't believe that I survived so many trials.

'Where are your travelling documents?' she asked.

I sighed.

'I have no travelling documents. The only piece of identity I have is my birth certificate.'

'So you are in Gabon without any papers?'

'Yes ma.'

'I'll take you to the authorities. I need to declare you as legal in this country.'

As I heard those words, I became afraid.

'No Mama Cathy,' I said. 'I may get into trouble.'

'No mon enfant, you'll not. From now on, you're my child. I'll not allow any harm to come to you. Not after all you've gone through.'

I was still extremely frightened and didn't know how the authorities might approach an illegal immigrant in their country attempting to seek residence. But Mama Cathy seemed so confident and so assured. It was almost as if she knew that I would be staying in Gabon. And she called me her son...The following day, we left to see the local authorities and seek advice. When we arrived at their office complex, Mama Cathy asked to speak to the chief immigration officer. Immediately, we were taken to his office. We sat down, while Mama Cathy explained the situation.

'C'est mon fils et je suis venu de lui faire officielle dans ce pays.'

'Que voulez-vous que je fasse madame?'

'Il a besoin d'un carte de séjour.'

'Est-il gabonais?'

'Non, il est Nigérian.'

'A-t-il une carte d'identité nationale ou un passeport Nigérian?'

'Non, il n'a que son certificat de naissance.'

'Ensuite, je suis désolé, parce que nous ne pouvons pas prendre sa requête sans cela.'

Hearing this, my heart sunk. I couldn't get a resident permit without a Nigerian identity card or passport. What could we do now? The officer conducted a little interview with me in English and concluded that he needed those details before he could process my resident permit.

'Merci. Nous allons obtenir ça bientôt,' Mama Cathy said.

When we left the office complex, I thought that we would be on our way home. To my surprise, Mama Cathy started pulling me in the opposite direction.

'All over today,' she repeated.

'Où allons-nous maintenant Mama Cathy?'

'You. Me. Ambassade du Nigeria.'

When we arrived at the Nigerian embassy, Mama Cathy spoke with them herself. A few minutes later, Mama Cathy came back with an immigration officer and gave me a date where I would have to come for an interview. Till the date of the interview, I was given a document that protected me from arrest. I was tremendously relieved; Mama Cathy was also happy. She had gotten what she wanted.

Three days later, I prepared myself for the interview. As I was about to leave the home, Mama Cathy shouted.

'Non, non, non. Nous voyageons ensemble. N'aller pas.'

I knew what *n'aller pas* meant: don't go. I went back into the living room, sat down and waited for Mama Cathy. When we arrived at the embassy, we were seen by the ambassador and a slender man called Miniru. He wore glasses, was about five feet tall and his suit accentuated his stockiness, while his shoes - freshly polished – presented a man of corporate professionalism. Upon instruction from the ambassador, Miniru dealt with everything we needed. A few hours later, I was issued with my first *laissez-*

passer, or identity card. I was officially registered as a Nigerian citizen.

Without delay, Mama Cathy and I made our way to the Gabonese local authorities. We showed them the identity card that had just been issued by the Nigerian embassy. To our shock, we were told that I needed an international passport before they could proceed with the issuance of the resident permit. Mama Cathy was infuriated. She explained how the chief immigration officer had only requested for either a resident permit or passport, but both were not told to be necessitated. We were both tired and it was getting late. There was nothing more we could do. Despite the disappointment of not obtaining the resident permit, I had got my identity card, which was a joy in itself. I thanked Mama Cathy a lot for what she did. She had really helped me. Soon after, we made our long journey back home.

The following day, Mama Cathy called the Nigerian ambassador and informed him of what the Gabonese local authorities had said. He was very upset and said he would try and get me an international passport as soon as he could. Mama Cathy thanked him; all we could do now was wait.

It had been a month since we were turned down by the Gabonese authorities, and French was slowly becoming easier to understand and speak. It was very early one morning when Mama Cathy called me.

'Mon enfant!' she shouted. 'Mon enfant!'

'Oui Mama Cathy, je viens.'

I went to Mama Cathy and sat by her with Mama Celine.

'My father's name is Arouna-Ndjom,' she began to tell me. 'Many years ago, Arouna came from Cameroon to look for a better life in Gabon. He was a hardworking man and tried very hard to become successful. While he was living in Gabon, he met a woman called Ayito and they both fell in love.'

'Your mother,' I responded.

'Yes. My father was a foreigner like you, but my mother's parents didn't want her to marry my father. My mother was a strong woman and would fight for what she wanted, but things went wrong.'

'What happened, Mama Cathy?'

'Well, my mother's parents gave Arouna and my mother a tough time. They were put through all sorts of trials, and my mother ended up becoming mentally ill. Meanwhile, my mother was pregnant with me. I was born on the first of January of the year 1943. After giving birth to me, I was taken away by my mother's parents, while my mother remained ill. I didn't know who my father was till I was six.'

'Really? How did you find out?'

'One day, I remember my father coming to visit my mother's family. He was chased away and called a stranger. Though at that time, I didn't understand why.'

'I'm so sorry to hear that.'

Mama Cathy went on.

'Four years later, at the age of ten, my great-uncle took me from primary school and sold me into marriage for about 20,000 CFA Francs, which was about US$40. I was sexually abused for four years...'

Mama Cathy couldn't withhold her tears and began to cry. I tried to console her, but her pain was evident to see.

'I couldn't bare it any longer,' she said. 'So I decided on a plan to run away. For almost two months I tried to figure out how I would escape. There was a large table near the entrance of the living room and right behind that was a door that led to freedom. Unfortunately, the door was always locked to prevent me from escaping. On that fateful day, someone opened the door and left it open. As they called my name and began looking for me inside, I ran away to my cousin's home.'

'Really?' I asked, in disbelief.

'My cousin disapproved of my early marriage and abuse and took me in. I lived with her until I was fifteen. Before I left, she put me into a paid job and soon after, I went in search of my father. I spent two weeks searching, before I finally found him. He was ill, disabled, and lonely.'

'I'm so sorry.'

'He was so happy to see me that day…if you saw his face. And I was so happy to see him for the first time in my life. Sadly, I was only able to see him for a few days longer.'

She wept and wept; I could only console her. The melancholy atmosphere was too much for me and a tear rolled down my cheek.

'After that, I went to look for my mother. She was so ill and looked tired. I took her away from where she was and tried to take care of her.'

There was a long pause.

'Now she is with me today. But I am lonely and have only been left with horrible memories that plague my mind from time to time. Because of the abuse I received, I could no longer have a child of my own. I lost hope in everything, until you came mon enfant.'

Listening to Mama Cathy's experience was humbling for me; it made the hairs on my skin bristle. Of course I was upset, but I was also happy for Mama Cathy. Although she went through tough trials herself, she survived. Everything she had gone through almost felt too woeful to be true, but Mama Cathy's story strengthened my resolve in life. Adversity will come; there should be no doubts about it. But it's how we cope and fight through adversity that defines us as a person. It's the experience that shapes us into what we become. It's our approach to it that tells us whether we will reach the end of the trial. That's why Mama Cathy's story helped me. Because it allowed me to appreciate that you never get anywhere you want in life by standing still and letting others dictate. You dictate; you decide.

There was a long silence after Mama Cathy spoke. Mama Celine who had sat and listened the whole way through could no longer hold back her tears. It's a story she must have listened to many times before, but the magnitude of the story was too strong for even her to survive its force.

It felt good to have shared my experience with Mama Cathy, especially after she had explained her life to me also. From then on, any awkwardness there once was dissipated. Mama Cathy was part of my life and I was part of hers. I was her family and she was mine. Sometimes, we would go to the farm together and while there we would say jokes and make each other laugh. We soon became a source of comfort for each other. Every time she called me *mon enfant*, I was proud to call her *mon mama*. The first time I said those words to her she smiled and repeated them.

'Mon mama,' she continued. 'I could get used to that.'

We laughed.

Five months later, on a fairly lukewarm morning in early 1988, I was sitting down on the dining table, eating breakfast when Mama Cathy spoke to me.

'Guess what?' Mama Cathy asked.

'What?'

'The Nigerian embassy called me yesterday. Your passport is ready.'

I couldn't believe what I was hearing. This was a moment of joy. I had begun to think that the passport wouldn't be done, but thankfully, I was proved wrong. The elation on my face glowed like a shining star. I was so thankful to Mama Cathy.

Three days later, Mama Cathy and I went to visit the local authorities again, after we had gone to collect my passport from the embassy. After three hours of waiting, I was issued with a *Carte de Séjour*. After near three years of residing in Gabon, I was issued a resident permit. It was almost like a dream. No more would I have to walk the other side of the pavement because a Gabonese gendarme was close-by, no more would I have to jump out of windows because of *contrôle*, no more would I have to pity myself because I couldn't get a job. Finally, I had a real ticket to freedom — a legal one. Everything happened so quickly that day; I was so thrilled. I hugged Mama Cathy and the immigration officer before falling to my knees where I buried my face in my hands, and began to cry. I couldn't believe it.

As I began to stand up, a tall figure towered over me. I raised my eyes to see who it was and once I had gotten a full view, my heart skipped a beat. History had a strange way of repeating itself or was it that the world was too small. Either way, I couldn't believe my eyes. Standing in front of me, with the same black suit he wore when he let us loose into Gabon, was the airport immigration manager. To my surprise, he remembered me.

'Are you not the young gentleman who washed my car?'

'Yes sir,' I replied.

'I used to work in this place,' he said.

There was a slight pause as he looked at me.

'How are you?'

'I'm fine sir.'

'You look scared.'

'Why wouldn't I be?' I thought.

The airport immigration manager took me outside the office complex and pointed towards the skies.

'It's such a beautiful day isn't it? Look at the way the bird flies high into the sky without a care in the world. Be happy, young man, because it's good to be free.'

'Thank you, sir,' I said in quick succession.

He smiled and walked back into the office. As he did, Mama Cathy was rushing towards me.

'Where did you go?'

'Nowhere. A man was talking to me.'

As we went home, Mama Cathy and I shared our excitement. I finally had my resident permit and I could finally start thinking about how to get a proper job and getting back into education. This was most definitely a new start in life; I had been given another chance. I was so grateful to Mama Cathy.

As we neared home, something the immigration manager said stuck to me.

'It's good to be free…it certainly is,' I thought.

Chapter 7: Running Away

Time moved incredibly fast. It was mid-1990, and I was approaching twenty years old. I was in my early adult years, yet it felt no different to before. Slowly, I was getting better at French. Mama Cathy had hired a Francophone teacher to help me. I was able to read and write French with much more ease, and it only strengthened communication between us. Soon, Mama Celine wouldn't be needed to translate. I worked with Mama Cathy a lot. She owned a lot of properties and an entire village, but I only realised this when we went on trips to collect rent from her tenants. I was living a settled life with Mama Cathy and we were both much happier.

I hadn't seen Texan for over two years now and I missed him dearly. We did keep in touch, but it was mostly through passed-on messages from the farm driver. He always said how he was keeping well and life was much more promising. I was happy for him; I only wished to see him again.

On a warm evening, we received a knock on our door. It was Texan! How happy I was to see him looking well and happy. Mama Cathy had never seen Texan before, but had only heard about him. He visited for two days before he left, but he promised to come back again soon. A week after Texan's departure, I received a letter from Mary.

Dear Peter, my son,

It's been quite some time since the last time you wrote me. I am worried about you. I hope you are well.

I told Tony that you wrote me a letter and have told him that you are now somewhere in Central Africa. He wasn't pleased at all. He said I was the one encouraging you and if anything bad happens to you, I would be responsible. But I think he misses you.

It has been over a year since I last saw your sister Joy, and that was just before her departure to Kano. Tony is still with Beki and the children, while I am in the village in Badagry.

You know I can't read or write, but I asked one of the village boys to help me write to you. What about your education? I hope you're now back at school?

I am always thinking of you son and I hope to see you soon. Write me back please my son. You know you're the only one I have.

Bye.

Your Mother,

Mary.

I was happy to hear from Mary, though I remember sending her a letter a few months ago. Perhaps she didn't receive it. I wondered why Joy was now living in Kano, a Northern state of Nigeria and hadn't visited Mary for over a year. I became upset and worried about her well-being. I hoped she was okay. I quickly wrote a letter back to Mary.

Once I had written the letter, I quickly went to post it. On my way home, Eko's taxi pulled up beside me. It had been almost three years since I last saw him. We were both delighted to see each other. Eko offered to take me home and I happily obliged. We had a long conversation in his taxi. It was good to see him again.

One day, I decided I would go to *marché Mont-Bouët* to purchase a few goods. It was the largest market in Gabon, with hundreds of stalls selling fruits, poultry, household goods, clothes and a variety of other goods. Most foreigners came to this market to trade, buy and sell goods. It was a busy market and always highly congested. Next to the market was a city motor park, or as we knew it, *Gare Routier*. On my visit through the market, I met a man called Mr Ayo Kalu. He was a marketer and goods supplier who would buy clothes and jewellery to sell and supply to marketers and local retailers. It looked like a profitable business and so I asked Mr Kalu if I could also become a trader. He accepted me and I soon became his apprentice.

As months continued to pass, Mr Kalu and I became very close. We were now heavily involved in buying and selling. At one point, Mr Kalu no longer treated me as his apprentice, but his partner. I was so grateful. He introduced me to countless customers and taught me how to order goods from overseas. We had to ensure what we ordered was in trade, in stock and in fashion — that was always important for Mr Kalu. We ordered menswear, womenswear, footwear, jewellery and traditional clothes amongst a whole list of other goods. During my time with Mr Kalu, I met a lot of traders and saved a lot of money. When I finally had enough money, I decided I would become an independent trader, though I would also be helping Mr Kalu.

After becoming an independent trader, I would begin to supply people, street shops, wholesalers and retailers with a variety of goods and products. My passion for trade grew. Every time I made a little more money, I would think of making even more and it would work. It was almost as if I couldn't stop multiplying my profit margins. The only problem was that I couldn't purchase goods abroad and bring them to Gabon. Although I was making a lot of money, purchasing goods overseas was too expensive even for me. You had to be someone like Mr Kalu to have enough risk bearing sums to purchase overseas. Staying local was good enough for me to raise enough money to get back into education. But I desired a business that would ensure I made money, and made it fast at that. After conducting some market research, I approached a block factory and enquired about how to make building blocks.

I asked Mama Cathy for a portion of land to help me build my small block factory. She agreed and gave me a place on the main road, which was in front of Mama Cathy's village at Lalala Golf. The land had a large amount of overgrowing vegetation that stood over seven feet tall. I immediately took to the grass with my cutlass. I ordered sand, bags of cement and gravel as well as moulds to produce the bricks. I also needed to employ a block-moulder. I soon met and employed a young man named Keita who lived in the neighbourhood and had experience with making blocks. Keita taught me how to make blocks. He worked as the block-moulder, while I was his labourer. He showed me how to adjust the ratios of sand, cement and gravel, which changed their hardness. As days continued, I was soon able to make blocks myself to Keita's approval. It was strenuous work, but also quite therapeutic. Gradually, the piece of land that was once solely a block factory also became an office. With the help of Mama Cathy's family friend, Mme Olga, I created a solid business. It was named Briketerie Ereb, after Mme Olga's company, Ereb Enterprises. I was proud of what I had created, especially at my age. When I went to work every day, I saw young Gabonese boys lazy or ashamed to work as a block-moulder, but doing nothing productive with their lives. Usually, they'd say things like *sale boulot* or dirty job. They thought of themselves as too posh to touch dirt, and considered public block-moulder men, like Keita and I, to be illiterate. In my mind, I simply laughed. I loved what I was doing.

Although Mama Cathy struggled to read and write, she was gifted with wisdom. She always persuaded me to get back to school, stating that she didn't want me to be like her. It was hard to find a school in Gabon as most schools taught in French. I didn't know what to do or where to start. But one day, I visited a local shop to buy some fitness magazines. I was reading through when I noticed an advertisement by a High School. They offered a correspondence course in security management. The desire to get back to school was so great that I decided I would join a course in the school. I sent a letter and two weeks later received a pack containing an application form. In four weeks, I had received practice test questions, the complete twelve module course pack and information about the cost of the course. After looking at all the information, I decided I would start the course to Mama Cathy's delight. At first, it was difficult for me to cope, especially because of my poor literacy levels and low confidence, but I was determined to not allow my past to plague my future. I began to balance my studies with work and was able to finish the first module within three weeks. I sent the module to the school in Brussels and received back a score of 90%. It was a remarkable result! I was so pleased, but also overwhelmed.

Although I was almost always either at the block factory or studying, I still made sure to visit Mr Kalu and help him. My visits were irregular, but Mr Kalu was patient with me and was always happy to see me. I also made sure that I dedicated Wednesdays to help Mama Cathy at the farm. My schedule was so busy that at times I didn't even have time to eat. I used to think of myself as a businessman or a trader, and my schedule certainly fitted the description, even if my attire didn't.

Mama Cathy was a marvellous woman, but she was strong and firm also. She was tough on certain issues and when she was angry you would know. Some people in the neighbourhood even named her: 'the hard woman' for the way that she acted at times. Tolerance was a quality any person living with Mama Cathy needed to have. Making silly mistakes, messing around and being lazy were not allowed. If you did all of those things, and she pointed it out to you, swallowing your pride and apologising were perhaps the best options. Over the years I learned that that was the best method for a lasting bond. Yet, even though she had these tendencies, Mama Cathy was hard-working, loving, generous, sociable and a champion of hospitality. Her kindness was great; she was truly a loving mother.

One day, late in the evening, Mama Cathy sat me down on her sofa and began speaking to me about challenging days ahead. She tenderly expressed herself.

'Mon enfant, you need to be strong. Life is full of challenges, but it's how positive we are to face those challenges that determine whether we succeed.'

Mama Cathy rarely spoke like this. I began to think that I had done something wrong or something was happening to her. She continued.

'My mother is mentally ill and my father was disabled. I witnessed my father's death before my very eyes. It was just me and him in the room. They were in pain when I was born and in pain when I grew up.'

I began to wonder what Mama Cathy was trying to tell me. I simply listened as she carried on.

'I was repeatedly raped by a man who was old enough to be my father and this man's wives turned me into a slave in their home. At ten years old, I wanted to die. My heart couldn't bear it any longer. But even though they may have succeeded in destroying my future, they never took away my hope.

The damage has been done, the repair has been difficult, but I want you to remember one thing from this.'

'What Mama Cathy?'

'Never stop doing good deeds to others because goodness will bring you joy.'

'Thank you Mama Cathy.'

Those words would never leave my memory; I treasured them greatly.

Mama Cathy had been an exceptional mother to me. Those words of wisdom and advice would be engraved in my heart. Although I had lost Elizabeth, Mama Cathy became a mother that any child would have dreamed to have. I was glad to have her, and I knew, deep down, she was glad to have me.

Months passed and I continued to juggle managing the block factory, working with Mr Kalu and helping Mama Cathy at the farm. While working with Mr Kalu one day, I met a man named Amos. He was a trader and often travelled abroad, buying and selling goods. He was a short man, friendly and gentle, with small lips and was extremely dark, like most of the Gabonese. I found out that Amos lived very close to where I lived in Lagos, and that he was also a tenant at Mama Cathy's village. I was hugely surprised as I had never met him before then. Nonetheless, it was good to speak with him. As the conversation grew, I learnt that Amos would be travelling to Nigeria very soon. This was great news. I asked Amos if he could help me deliver a letter and some money I intended to send to Mary in the village. Without hesitation, Amos accepted. He spent two weeks in Gabon before departing.

Amos returned after a month in Nigeria. Fortunately, I caught him outside his door late in the evening.

'Hi Amos.'

'Hi Peter.'

'You're back!'

'Yeah, I arrived yesterday night. How are you?'

'I'm good thanks. How's Nigeria?'

'It was cool man. It was cool.'

'That's good to hear. By the way, were you able to deliver my letter?'

'Yes. Actually, I was going to see you tomorrow about it. But since you're here, I'll tell you now.'

'Oh great.'

'I delivered the letter to a boy called Jack,' he continued. 'The boy promised to go to the village the next day. I'm sorry I wasn't able to do it myself. It's just that I had only two days left before I had to leave the city.'

Amos didn't see Mary, and there was just something about him that told me he wouldn't. I wasn't entirely pleased as it meant I couldn't get an immediate response or reaction from Mary, but at least he met Jack. Amos told me he would be visiting Nigeria again in two weeks, and would check if the message was delivered. I wrote another letter just in case and gave it to him. It was simply time to wait.

'Not again,' I thought. 'She just doesn't get it. I've explained to her on countless occasions that my priority is my job. I don't need to be distracted.'

As soon as I reached twenty, she did anything and everything to confront me. Jessica. Jessica. Jessica.

'Mon enfant, what do you think of Jessica?'

'I don't think about her, so I wouldn't really know.'

'A blunt response,' I thought. 'Perhaps that will put off another question.'

'Don't you think she is a beautiful girl with such good character?'

Mama Cathy would not relent. When she was on a mission, it would be completed — no matter what the cost.

'Looking at her for a second, at any one time in two to three weeks, wouldn't really put me in a great position to answer that question.'

'I'm glad you're not a stand-up comedian,' she cynically retorted. 'Your jokes would make no one laugh.'

'I'm glad too because I wasn't joking.'

We both began to laugh. There was a small silence.

'You know I want the best for you,' she solemnly expressed. 'Don't you think I need to hear the cry of a new-born child under my roof?'

'Mama Cathy,' I sternly replied. 'Honestly, I couldn't care less if Jessica is of good character or not. I'm not ready for marriage now. Besides, I don't really like her, if I've even thought about liking her. What about my work and study? Have you thought about that?'

'Yes, of course. While married, you can do those things at the same time. Have *you* not thought about that?'

'I don't want to be distracted, mama. I know you want me to have a child under your roof, but I'm just not ready.'

'You don't have to be ready. I will take care of the child for you, while you can carry on doing whatever you do.'

'Hahaha, very funny Mama Cathy. Change topic.'

For months Mama Cathy would relentlessly badger me about getting married. She just wouldn't give up.

One weekend, Mama Cathy was busy in the kitchen cooking what she called 'a special meal'. She wouldn't let me enter the kitchen for the whole day; not even to take bread. Usually I'd force my way through, but I decided not to because the aromas that left the kitchen scintillated my taste buds and made me crumble like a biscuit. I'd wait.

'It's good food,' I thought. 'I'll wait.'

Late that evening, someone knocked on the door. Mama Cathy asked me to let the visitor in. It was Jessica! I couldn't believe it, but it all began to make sense. The 'special meal' Mama Cathy was talking about was for Jessica and me. She had invited Jessica to have dinner with us that night. I invited Jessica to sit, and as I did, I heard someone else knock on the door. Mama Cathy had invited more people over.

'Thank goodness for that,' I thought.

I don't think I would have been able to survive if it was just Mama Cathy, Jessica and I. All I had to do was survive the night without provoking Mama Cathy. I showed no attention to Jessica. After some time, Mama Cathy asked Jessica a question.

'My daughter, what do you think of my son?'

Jessica laughed without uttering a word.

'Good response,' I thought.

'Don't worry I understand,' Mama Cathy replied.

As the night progressed, I began to think whether this was Mama Cathy's plan to bring Jessica and me together. I wasn't happy. I didn't love Jessica and I wasn't ready for marriage. Why was Mama Cathy forcing me? I wished no longer to be part of the night. Before everyone left, I went to speak with Mama Cathy.

'I need to see someone on the road. I will see you later.'

'No Peter. Wait a bit more. Please, you will see Jessica out. It is quite late and after that you can go and do whatever you ostensibly want to do.'

I had a funny feeling that Mama Cathy would ask me to do something like that, but I couldn't say no. Mama Cathy was my mother. I was always taught to 'obey before complain'. But for those few minutes, I hated that rule.

Thirty minutes later, Jessica told Mama Cathy she was leaving. As asked, I saw Jessica off till she went into a taxi. There was an awkward tension that hung in the air like the vile stench of faeces that you desperately want to clear, but have to wait till nature takes it proper course. But I was determined not to say a single word.

Walking her out, however, allowed me to observe Jessica's beauty for the first time. Jessica really was beautiful as Mama Cathy had said. She was slim, healthy, of average height, had long hair and a warm smile, but even though she possessed all that beauty, I wasn't attracted to her.

As Jessica entered the taxi, I spoke.

'Bye Jessica.'

'Bye Peter.'

The taxi drove off into the night.

'Job done,' I thought.

Although Jessica seemed like a nice person, I wasn't ready for marriage. I was still trying to forget about my past and move on with my life. For the first time in my life, I was settled. I had a job, and I was happy. I didn't need anything to distract me or disrupt my life. I simply was not ready yet. When I got home, I expected Mama Cathy's questions.

'How did it go? What did you say to her? Does she like you?'

A series of questions in quick succession; my brain couldn't handle it.

'C'mon Mama Cathy, one question at a time.'

'Okay then, what happened?'

'Nothing. I didn't say a word. Well apart from 'Bye', but I guess that doesn't really count, does it?'

'What? You didn't say a word to her!'

'I told you I never liked her, but you've kept forcing me.'

'That's okay.'

'Seriously?'

'I will talk to her myself. In fact, I will marry her for you.'

And as she said those words, she walked off.

'Mama Cathy! I said I don't like her!'

She shut her room door behind her.

How was I going to cope with Mama Cathy? Jessica wasn't even the problem. What was I going to do?

A month later, Amos had arrived from his journey. After a few days, I went to visit him.

'Hi Amos!'

'Hi Peter! How are you?'

'I'm good thanks, were you able to see Mary this time?'

I didn't hesitate to ask Amos the question I really wanted an answer to.

'Yes! In fact, I went to your village and delivered your message personally. Mary told me she didn't receive the other message and I couldn't explain why. Anyway, here is a letter she sent you.'

'Thanks Amos! You're a good friend!'

I took the letter from Amos' hands and rushed home. I opened the letter and read slowly and carefully. Mary was well, but complained that she wanted to see me soon. She hadn't heard from Joy for three years since she had left the city, and she didn't have an address. At least Mary was safe and well. I smiled; at least there was some happiness to be had amidst the stress Mama Cathy was ceaselessly hurling upon me.

'I also hope to see you soon too, mum,' I thought.

A few weeks later, it was late in the afternoon when I heard Mama Cathy speaking with someone in her room. I was going to tell her that I had come in early from work, but as I entered her room, I quickly attempted to depart.

'Peter, Peter. Come.'

I reluctantly obliged.

'Have you seen Jessica?'

'Until now…no.'

'She is here to see you. I think both of you will make a good couple. What do you think Peter?'

I couldn't bear it any longer.

'Hello Jessica, could I please have a word with you outside?'

Jessica followed me outside Mama Cathy's room.

'I'm so sorry. You're a nice girl, but this is purely Mama Cathy's idea. I am not ready for a relationship. I hope you understand.'

She didn't say a word. I felt terrible having to do this, but Mama Cathy had created this. It wasn't fair that she had to go through this.

'Mama Cathy wants children, but what happened to love?'

Jessica still didn't say a word.

'Please let her know that you're not interested too, so that she will leave me alone. Please.'

'But I like you. Mama Cathy asked if I do, and I said "Yes".'

I couldn't believe my ears.

'Oh, so this was your idea?'

'No, Mama Cathy started everything.'

I could not allow this to go on any longer.

'Jessica, let me be frank. I'm not interested in a relationship.'

'But I like you and I'm in love with you.'

I could sense her emotion by the trembling modulation of her voice. Perhaps, this had come to her as a major blow, but it had to be done. Mama Cathy had allowed Jessica to think I liked her, but Jessica's eyes yearned for a favourable reply. She looked pitiful. I was confused; I didn't know whether to accept my fate. After all, Jessica was of good character and beautiful. Was Mama Cathy right in her actions? Did Jessica really deserve to go through this? As I began to create feelings for her, I reluctantly moved away. I couldn't allow myself to be confused.

I had developed a huge motherly affection for Mama Cathy and I didn't want to offend her, especially after all she had done for me. I knew she wanted children, but I didn't want to enter a situation where I would regret my actions in the future. My heart was troubled and all I desired was for the Jessica dilemma to end.

Weeks passed and Mama Cathy didn't bother me about Jessica. Perhaps she had finally realised that forcing me to marry Jessica wasn't a good idea. After the Jessica dilemma, my horrific nightmares returned. I just couldn't get away from my past. As they say, 'you can run, but you can't hide'.

Chapter 8: The Daughter of Mr Babela

'I'm just getting fed up with these things. I wasn't ready for it,' I explained.

'I understand Peter,' replied Texan. 'I'm even confused. Mama Cathy thinks I was the one encouraging you to reject Jessica's proposal and I wasn't even here all this time.'

We both laughed.

'Even if I want to get married, I'm grown enough to make my own choices. Besides, I don't want to be distracted,' I said.

It was early 1992 and I was 21 years old. Texan had only arrived that night and I had already begun to hurl upon him the incidents that had taken place after his last visit. Texan stayed for three weeks before returning back to his village. It was always good to have him around.

Two months after Texan's departure, Mama Cathy and I went to a gathering with friends. During the gathering, I came across a tall man. His name was Jean Bosco, or as he was nicknamed Jibé. He was wearing a black suit, with a white shirt and yellow tie. Jibe had a rectangular face and his face was quite dark, meaning that at times, his eyes would appear to be hidden. His hair, unlike most Africans, was not jet black. Instead, it was scattered with white hairs. Moreover, his tough skin and wrinkled forehead presented to me a man of older years. He had incredibly broad shoulders which meant that the suit he wore made his upper body rather rectangular. His young and strong stance contradicted his facial features. After inquiring, I found out he was only in his mid-thirties. Jibé originated from Zaire, now known as the Democratic Republic of

Congo, and hardly spoke any English. But after the gathering Jibé and I became close friends.

We became good friends over the following months. One day, while I was on my way to visit Jibé, my eyes caught sight of the eighth wonder of the world. Her hair was a rich shade of ebony, and I watched it flow gracefully over her glowing sepia-like skin. Her eyes, hazel and young, radiated brighter than the stars. She had a small, elegant, button-like nose and her full lips had a rose tint. Any person would have thought they had gone to heaven, but I guess heaven had been brought to me. She was wearing a yellow dress, which made it feel like sunshine had been brought back into my life. I looked to the heavens and simply thought: what did I do to deserve this? Everything about her was stunning. She moved with grace and she raised her arms in a charming, but almost beguiling manner. My eyes were fixated on her; I began to daydream.

Jibé nudged me.

'Peter, are you okay?'

'I've been blessed,' I continued. 'Look at her Jibé! She's the quintessential manifestation of perfection.'

'I never knew you could say so many big words…'

There was a pause.

'You're crazy! Please don't tell me you're attracted to her.'

'I think I'm in love,' I said. 'What's her name?'

Jibé laughed, but it was almost mocking.

'Her name, you deranged human being, is M'bembi Bibiche Babela…the daughter of Jean Mukoko Babela.'

I was out of my trance.

'Why did you suddenly pause then put an emphasis on "daughter of Jean Mukoko Babela"?'

'I'm telling you now. Forget it. Don't even try it. There are many more fish in the sea, but this fish…is too big.'

'Look at my muscles Jibé. No fish is too big for me.'

'Peter, please don't tell me you are attracted to her?'

'No, I'm not attracted.'

'Good, let's keep on walking.'

We began to walk.

'I'm past that stage…I'm in love.'

Jibé looked into my face and shook his head.

As soon as I took sight of M'bembi, it was like I had met her before. M'bembi lived with her father and three sisters, while her mother lived in Zaire. But she hoped to join them soon. Jibé informed me that the bond between Jean and M'bembi was great and no man dared to speak with his daughter about love. But I was in love with M'bembi and I was positive she shared the same feelings. The way she looked at me proved it, or was I being naïve?

'Would Mama Cathy support me in my endeavour for M'bembi?' I pondered. 'Not with Jessica still alive.'

But perhaps I had started thinking of love too soon. At the end of the day, I had rejected Jessica because of that same reason and it had only been a few months since the incident. And what would happen to my ambitions, school and work?

'Never mind,' I thought. 'What did Mama Cathy say? You can do those things and still be in love.'

I decided to see M'bembi, but I was too afraid to speak with her. My French, although better, was nowhere near romantic. After much thinking, I decided to send her a love letter; though it was far from conventional.

O M'bembi!

How beautiful you are, my darling! Oh, how beautiful! Your eyes are doves. Strengthen me with raisins; refresh me with apples, for I am faint with love! Your cheeks are beautiful with earrings, your neck with strings of jewels. O M'bembi! You are radiant and ruddy, outstanding among ten thousand.

But you are my dove, my perfect one, unique, the favourite of the one who bore you. The young women see you and called you blessed; the men praise you. Come away, my beloved, and be like a gazelle on the spice-laden mountains of love! All beautiful you are, my darling; there is no flaw in you.

Place me like a seal over your heart, like a seal on your arm; for love is as strong as death, its jealousy unyielding as the grave. It burns like blazing fire, like a mighty flame.

Surging waters cannot extinguish love, nor can rivers wash it away. No man can come between my love for you.

Come now M'bembi! Hurry, my dear one, and be swift like a gazelle. I await you upon the mountain of spices!

Hoping to read from you soon. You can send a reply through my friend, Jibé.

Truly yours I remain,

Peter.

Inspired by the Songs of Solomon, I poured out my heart to M'bembi. I had never been in love before, but the feeling was incredulous. I wrote parts of the letter in French and English. Once I had finished writing and sealed it with a kiss, I gave it to Jibé to hand it to M'bembi. Although it was hard to express myself, I did the best I could to convey my thoughts. M'bembi was the first girl in my life that I had felt feelings for. Solomon was a powerful writer; I just hoped she understood what I meant.

A week passed and I had not received a reply from M'bembi. I could wait no longer. Jibé and I decided to visit her. Jibé was a friend of the Babela family, so it was easy for him to drop in and say hello. The visit was great and I was able to see M'bembi. Jean was not home so I was unable to see him. During the visit, I noticed M'bembi constantly looking in my direction. I could sense she liked me and from that day on, we both fell in love with each other.

M'bembi was about eighteen years old when we started seeing each other. She had three brothers (Phineas, Jonathan and Rufus) and three sisters (Tichou, Sulamite and Benoni). She was Jean's second child.

Sometimes, M'bembi would come and visit me at the block factory before she went home or she'd send me a love letter through Jibé, her sisters Sulamite and Benoni or her cousin, Audrey. Everyone wanted M'bembi and me to be together everyone except Jean. Occasionally, Jibé and I would go to a small market in Lalala to meet M'bembi or I would go alone. M'bembi would be at the market selling Congolese manioc prepared by her mother. But some days, M'bembi wouldn't be at the market, so she'd have to send a note through her sisters to let me know.

One day, I visited the market to see M'bembi. As I turned left onto the main stretch of the market, I saw Jean on the opposite sidewalk. M'bembi was only a few hundred yards away from me, yet, I knew if I approached her, there'd be a huge incident. Instinctively, as he looked in my direction, I turned my head away. A few seconds after, he carried on walking. I wasn't sure if he had spotted me, but it was certainly a close call. The third day after my little encounter with Jean, we were meant to gather at our place of worship where I'd be able to see M'bembi and we could discuss a better place to meet. Usually, she'd arrive with her family, but that day she didn't come. Shocked that something may have happened, I asked Sulamite what had happened. Instantly, she gave me a note.

Peter,

I saw you leave the market the other day and I think my father saw you too. I think he's pretending he hasn't, because all of a sudden he seems to be watching me everywhere I go. Please don't come to the market to see me anymore. I will write you again soon.

M'bembi,

Your love.

M'bembi warned me of her father's character and how disapproving he would be of our relationship and I likewise explained how antipathetic Mama Cathy would be. M'bembi and I were both chaste and wanted to remain so till marriage. I was extremely proud to hear her tell me this, especially since it was common for young people to engage in extramarital affairs, which they'd later regret in the future. For the moment, M'bembi and I both decided to keep our relationship a secret. We didn't want to raise any unnecessary attention or tension.

Weeks passed and my relationship with M'bembi grew stronger and stronger. But Jibé wasn't happy with where M'bembi and I were meeting and so he arranged a different meeting point, far away from Jean and Mama Cathy. Jibé arranged a place in Sogatol that belonged to a woman called Mama Sophie. Mama Sophie was married with two kids called Matina and Tibo. She was a kind woman and M'bembi and I decided to meet every Friday at her place in Sogatol, which was at least eight miles away from Mama Cathy's and Jean's homes. We would spend a lot of time at Mama Sophie's, where our love continued to grow.

M'bembi fluently spoke Lingala, a Bantu language largely spoken across northwestern Zaire. M'bembi would sometimes teach me a few words in Lingala when we were together. Often, she would send notes with a few words in Lingala. Within a few days, I knew food was *biloko*, water was *mayi* and give me water was *pesagayi mayi*. She would also end her letters in: *na lingi yo*, which meant I love you. It was quite fun learning Lingala; M'bembi and I shared a few laughs mocking my pronunciation.

One Friday, while leaving Mama Sophie's place, I met Jean formally face-to-face. Jean was a short, stocky man who was in his mid-forties. His immensely dark skin, blended in with his hair, so that his white eyes gave a stark contrast. He was casually dressed, with denim jeans and a plain red shirt. He held on a strong gaze, which suggested he was a deep thinker. He was standing at Mama Sophie's main gate. M'bembi and Jibé were still inside Mama Sophie's home and I desperately wanted to warn M'bembi of her father's presence. But if I re-entered that might reveal what he may already know. I decided to keep on walking. I greeted him with a glancing hello and walked out, pretending I was simply a visitor.

I wasn't sure if he'd answered me, but with just a little glimpse at his face, it was clear he was unhappy about something. Immediately, as I began to walk away, Jean marched into Mama Sophie's home. My heart jumped. I just couldn't think about what would happen when Jean found M'bembi at Mama Sophie's place, especially with me. A few hours later, Jibé visited me.

'Too close,' he said. 'Too, too close.'

I had managed to survive; Jean had not found out about our relationship.

Our rendezvous for the following week was cancelled because M'bembi and I weren't sure whether we were being watched by Jean.

Usually, when M'bembi and I met at Mama Sophie's place we would hide in a blind-spot that was at a sharp turning to Mama Sophie's room. That day, once Jean had walked in, he didn't greet Mama Sophie and her husband. Instead, he went straight to our little blind spot! Hearing the story, I couldn't believe it. Fortunately, Udoh, Mama Sophie's husband, had moved M'bembi into their room. But the intelligence Jean had to go straight to our blind spot was unbelievable. From then on, I knew it wouldn't be easy trying to persuade Jean to let me see his daughter. On leaving Mama Sophie's home, he was largely upset. Thankfully, he had failed.

Later that night, I received a note from M'bembi:

Mon amour, I miss you, je suis fou amoureuse de toi.

After reading her message, I also wrote a note and gave it to Jibé before he left my home. Jibé spoke.

'I am now a love messenger. Please call me not Jibé. My name is Jibé, the love messenger.'

'Then you're doing your job well.'

We both laughed.

Chapter 9: Where Are You From?

It was early 1993, and by now I was twenty two years old. M'bembi and I were practically inseparable, and as the days went on our love grew stronger. 'Peter,' she said, 'I want you to meet my parents formally.'

'She can't be serious,' I thought.

'You and I both know that that's not possible. Your father will oppose it and who knows what Mama Cathy will say?'

'I've written to my mother about it,' she explained. 'I've told her how much I love you and she's happy that I've found someone. And if you really do love me, you should make your intentions known.'

'M'bembi, you know that I love you, but it's too early. What if things go wrong?'

I began to sound like the ultimate pessimist.

'Don't worry. My mother will be returning from Zaire soon and she'll be able to handle my father.'

M'bembi's love for me could be seen by everyone who knew us. M'bembi and I were led to believe that Jean had suspicions about us, but he hadn't spoken a word to us yet. Perhaps he was playing along with us; I couldn't quite figure out why he didn't ask us whether any of the rumours were true. But I was also worried about Mama Cathy and whether she would support me. As days passed, M'bembi was forcing me to speak to her parents. She wanted us to get married, but I didn't know what to do. I was confused.

A few months later, M'bembi's mother arrived from Zaire. Days after her arrival, I received a note through Jibé. It was Josephine, M'bembi's mother. She'd invited me to their home the very next day. I was apprehensive, not least because of Jean's reaction to my affection for M'bembi.

'Jibé, I don't think I'm going to go.'

'What d'you mean you're not going? She insisted that you must,' Jibé continued. 'Besides I'm going with you and the woman knows what she's doing.'

'Are you sure?'

'Yes, yes. Relax Peter. It'll be fine.'

'If you say so.'

The next day, Jibé and I went to M'bembi's home. M'bembi had gone out and, fortunately, Jean was not present. Relief swarmed me knowing that I would be asked too many serious or harsh questions. But I didn't really know what to expect from Josephine either. We spent a few hours talking to Josephine and the visit went well. I soon realised that Josephine simply wanted to meet me and know who I was.

Over time, Josephine and I developed a cordial relationship. She was in full support of me courting M'bembi. Because of Jibé, I was able to walk in and out of the Babela home as I liked, and at times I would see Jean. I think he knew what was going on because he would always give me a funny look while I was there, but he didn't say anything to me or about the matter. My relationship with M'bembi was unbreakable. As soon as I gazed my eyes upon her, I knew she was the one I truly loved. Everything seemed to be going well, until one Saturday evening when I was invited to M'bembi's home.

'Peter, I believe you must see Jean and let him know your intentions towards our daughter, M'bembi,' Josephine said.

I remained silent. The thought of speaking with Jean was petrifying in itself. I didn't know how he would react to me being in a relationship with his daughter. Perhaps he was so silent for so long because he didn't allow himself to believe what was happening.

Josephine continued.

'I know what you are thinking, but you have to see him… sooner rather than later.'

Earlier Jibé informed me that Jean believed that M'bembi and I were hiding something from him and he was determined to find out. But Josephine's next words would confirm this.

'I am almost certainly sure he is fully aware that your feet are in our home because of M'bembi.'

'Okay, I will try and do something about it,' I replied.

In reality, however, what could I really do? I didn't know how I would approach him and what he would say. Would he like me? Would he be angry that I had not told him that I was dating his daughter? There were so many thoughts, but equally, there were also so many questions. I decided to speak to one of my closest friends, Pierre Essengone, or as he was nicknamed Fefe. Fefe had an oblong face, with angular cheekbones, a slightly curved chin, and a sturdy jaw line. His small eyes were a raven black and his slick eyebrows followed the curvature of his frontal bone. He had a broad, rounded African nose that hung above his thin, straight lips. His hair was jet black, freckled with white hairs, but always combed and never one hair out of place. He was a tall man, with broad shoulders and was always seen in a shirt and tie. His natural authority was palpable, his experiences evident in his speech and his calmness always identified by his steady gaze.

I arranged a meeting with Fefe, to explain the situation with M'bembi and I to him. Fefe was a good friend to Jean so I thought it was best to seek advice from him about how to approach Jean. When I had finished outlining the problem to Fefe, he spoke.

'We all know you are in a relationship with M'bembi. Jean knows, but he has not seen anything disconcerting to approach you about. So he deliberately kept himself quiet. But I tell you now, it will not be easy.'

It brought me great relief when Fefe promised to try and have a profound and amiable discussion with Jean about the matter. We spoke about the day he would have the meeting and before departing, Fefe spoke.

'One step at a time, Peter.'

I didn't know what Fefe meant.

'I don't get it,' I replied.

'Do not let Mama Cathy know about this yet or things could get really bad.'

'Okay Fefe.'

Two weeks later, late in the afternoon, Fefe invited me to his home.

'Peter,' he said. 'I tried my best, but he insisted. He doesn't want you to be in a relationship with his daughter. He said he would never let you marry any of his children.'

I couldn't believe what I was in hearing. Before I could speak, Fefe continued.

'But the worst thing is…'

Fefe paused.

'What happened?'

'The reason is because he said that he would never let a Nigerian marry his daughters.'

'This is ridiculous,' I thought.

'And he's also promised to visit you at your home this evening.'

I jumped up from my chair.

'What?!'

'Sit down, sit down,' Fefe said waving his hands up and down.

'Why does he want to visit me? Why?'

'I'm not entirely sure, but I think he wants to warn you.'

'Warn me?'

'Yes, to tell you never to see his daughter again.'

'Well, he won't see me here,' I explained. 'I'm going out. I don't want Mama Cathy to know what is going on.'

I loved M'bembi wholeheartedly. I had given her everything that I could have, and now her father was telling me we couldn't be together. Disappointment and frustration were not strong enough to describe the feelings I was experiencing. What was wrong with Nigerians? Or was this just an excuse because he didn't like me? I simply didn't understand. After staying out for a while, I returned home. I asked Jibé to keep me company as I desperately needed someone to speak with. Two hours later, I heard a knock on the door. I thought it was Mama Cathy and went to open the door.

'You! You! Stay away from my daughter!' Jean acrimoniously shouted.

Jean looked like he had been possessed. He was yelling profusely.

'Papa, calm down.'

'Don't tell me to calm down! And never call me Papa again!'

Jibé intervened.

'Uncle, please. Come inside. Don't do this. Look, people are looking at us. Let us go in.'

'Jibé don't involve yourself. Or you think I don't know you have been passing love letters to my daughter from this fool,' Jean said pointing at me.

'Sorry sir,' I replied.

'You'd better be sorry, and as for my daughter, never speak to her again! In fact, never set your eyes on her again. Over my dead body will I allow a Nigerian to marry my daughters!'

Outside my door, we had received an audience. I was being humiliated. I couldn't say a word. Jibé tried to clear the crowd, while I went inside. What had I done to deserve this?

The following day M'bembi visited me.

'What do you want from me?' I asked. 'Your father has warned me to stay away from you. Besides, I need time to think about what's happened. Please, go.'

'No,' she protested. 'I'm not going anywhere.'

'Your father has come in between us. I don't want to cause you any trouble and I don't want to give myself any trouble or upset Mama Cathy. So go, please.'

'But I just told you I'm not going anywhere!'

There was a pause.

'Do you still love me Peter?'

'Yes, of course I do. But if your father sees you here, I'm dead.'

'Then why are you being so harsh? You're acting like I wasn't warned by my father as well. He's not even speaking to my mother because of us.'

'That's exactly what I'm saying. I'm just trying to save us both from the wrath of your father. We can't be together for now and we both know it. Your father doesn't like me, so please. I don't want to cause you any more grief.'

'I promise you my father will regret this.' Tears began to drop from M'bembi's eyes. 'I will go, but on one condition.'

'What condition?'

She didn't answer my question.

'Just tell me you love me.'

'Yes, of course I do. We just have to wait a little. Let some air steam.'

M'bembi refused to tell me the condition. After our conversation, M'bembi tearfully left me. From that day onwards, M'bembi would occasionally send me letters via Jibé. A month later, M'bembi visited me.

'But I told you to stay away for the time being.'

'I know. I know,' she explained. 'I'm only here for a short visit. My father saw the letter I was about to send you and is threatening to send me back to Zaire. We had a serious fight and I'm scared he might do something to you he'll regret. So I agree with you, let's keep away from the time being. As for my father, he will positively regret his actions.'

I didn't know what to make of it. We were letting each other go for the moment, but wouldn't that pull us away from each other? Was this how our relationship would collapse?

I held her hands and looked into her eyes.

'You know my love for you cannot be measured?'

'I will never marry anyone else. I only love you.'

Soon after, M'bembi left me. I didn't know when I would see her again and Jean was tightening his grip on our relationship. The uncertainty was taunting me; Jean had got his way.

Chapter 10: A Rose Petal

I hadn't seen M'bembi for months. Time transpired quickly and the fervency I once had to return to school was gradually eroding. I became more and more committed to my work, and eventually became a workaholic. Perhaps I fell back on my work to come to terms with my break away from M'bembi, but a distraction was exactly what I needed.

During this time, Mary wrote to me regularly, asking about my wellbeing and whether I had returned back to education. It was mostly because of her letters that my mind would wander to whether I would ever return. She would also write about Joy and the fact she hadn't returned or sent a single letter. I hadn't seen Mary for a lengthy period of time, so I began considering whether this would be an appropriate time to visit her. It would draw me away from the current troubles of Gabon and give me some breathing space. I spent almost a week debating whether I should return to Nigeria, but eventually, I decided I would.

I began preparing my journey back to Nigeria. If I was to leave the country, I required a visa to travel. This was all novel to me. It was obligatory for foreigners that resided in Gabon to obtain an *Autorisation Sortie-Retour*, or permission to leave and return. It was a rather exciting experience planning my journey back to Nigeria and I was extremely grateful to the Gabonese authorities for granting me my first visa. Mama Cathy was also incredibly supportive, as she ardently desired for me to visit Mary again.

Perhaps I was so overwhelmed with the thought of travelling that I unremittingly annoyed my friends with talk of visiting overseas. Usually, Jibé would sit down watching the TV, while I explained my preparations and when I'd ask him if he was paying attention, he'd nod his head very slowly. Only now do I realise that he never really was paying any attention.

Approaching Libreville Leon M'ba Airport, I strode across the ground with bullish confidence. Wearing a pair of fashionable grey jeans and a voguish jacket, I smiled at almost everything. I felt like royalty. As I strolled around the airport, every person I met or spoke to, I would give a winning smile and say 'Bonjour'. Likewise, they would reply 'Bonjour Monsieur' and return the smile. After my gallivanting adventure across my newly discovered kingdom, I sat down and watched the planes depart from Leon M'ba Airport. It was a stunning, breath-taking experience; I took the time to imagine exactly how I would feel when I would take that wondrous flight into the bright blue skies. After going through the boarding gate, I entered the plane and sat down. A few minutes passed, and the plane began to move slowly. Quicker than I had noticed, we had risen into the sky. I looked out of the window.

'Goodbye Gabon,' I whispered. 'See you soon.'

It was late at night when I arrived at Murtala Muhammed International Airport. I needed to get home quickly and rest, especially after the tiring, but fascinating plane trip. After looking around, I soon met a taxi driver. Though I never found out his real name, his nickname was 1020 because of the registration number on his taxi. Soon, we would be driving through the pitch black night of Lagos. If Lagos looked beautiful in the day, it looked majestic at night. After an hour's driving from the airport, we arrived in Ojo Local Government. Ojo is a local municipality located along Badagry Expressway in Lagos. I hoped to pass the remainder of the night with my brother Vincent.

Vincent lived in a boys' quarters, a colloquial name given to where servants and slaves would reside. Common to most homes in the city, the bathroom and toilet were located outside the quarters. His quarter was decrepit and in need of repairs, but it was manageable and it would be where I would spend most of my time while in Nigeria. Unsurprisingly, Vincent had changed significantly since we last met. I was elated to see him again and the joy on his face was easy to see. He thought I was dead, and the regular glances over his shoulder perhaps were reassuring him that I was real, even if I was a ghost from the past.

The very next morning, I made plans to see Mary. Vincent and I made our way to Akarakunmo. After so many years away, I was returning to the place where I'd grown up. I was nervous to say the least, but I was also looking forward to seeing Mary. I couldn't wait. As our car drove through the village, the day of the fire, the day I ran away from home and memories of the party all returned to me. Although these things may have beset my childhood, it was good to be home once again. It was good to be back.

Arriving at Mary's door, I was extremely nervous. I asked Vincent to knock. A few seconds later, the door opened.

'Mama,' Vincent said. 'I'm here with a friend. We were just passing by and I thought we might say hello.'

Mary hadn't seen me yet. Already turning her back, she let us in. Vincent asked me to sit down in the living room, while Mary had gone into the kitchen to grab some water.

'Wow!' I thought. 'The living room hasn't changed much.'

'She hasn't recognised me yet,' I told Vincent.

'No. But wait till she comes back. I'd love to see her reaction then.'

A few minutes later, Mary came back with glasses of water in her hand. She gave one glass to Vincent, and then approached me. She also gave me my glass of water; I quickly put it down.

'Thank you mama.'

'You're welcome my son…'

Mary paused.

'That's funny you sound like my son Peter.'

She looked into my eyes…and screamed.

'Peter! Peter! You came back! Why didn't you tell me?'

Hugging me, she was ecstatic. Vincent was laughing. Mary couldn't quite believe I was there and neither could I. It was all too dreamlike. Mary had aged a lot since I'd left and she looked very weak. But the delight on her face was indescribable. She began to touch my ears, my hair, my nose and my eyes. She felt the palm of my hands and whispered in my ear.

'Speak to me my son.'

I whispered back in her ear.

'I'm home mama.'

Tears rolled down her frail cheeks. Wiping them, I spoke.

'Don't cry mama. I'm home now. Don't cry.'

'I thought I'd never see you again Peter. I'm tired and getting weaker by the day. No one comes to visit except Tai and Janet, and sometimes Vincent. Peter, why did you leave me? Why?'

She began to weep heavily and rested her head in my shoulders.

'I'm sorry mama. I'm sorry.'

I held her and consoled her. I was truly back home.

I spent a few hours at Mary's home. We talked about a lot of things, but I was just happy that I was able to see her again. After spending some time with Mary, I made my way around the village.

I met Tai and Janet. They too had changed a lot. We began to reminisce about when we were younger; how we used to make sandcastles in the sand in Mary's front garden or how we would bathe ourselves in sand. And then while we were playing in the sand, we would hear the roaring engines of an aeroplane fly above, but it'd be the tiniest dot in the sky, and as it passed we would sing a song in Yoruba:

Aeroplane o dabọ
Ba mi ki iya mi eleko
Eko meji ranṣẹ si mi
O yó mi O yó mi
Mo ri ẹmo Agege
Aja we wu
O ro sọ
O wọ bata ẹsẹ kan

Clap Clap Hey Hey x2

Aeroplane goodbye
Greet my mother who sells eko
Send two ekos to me
I'm satisfied I'm satisfied
I saw something unusual in Agege
A dog wore clothes
It dressed in a wrapper
It wore a shoe on one foot

I stayed overnight with Mary. The following morning I tried to keep the conversation with Mary brief. I knew she would have a lot to tell me, but I wanted to speak to her later. I needed to see certain people while I was still in Nigeria. I made my way to Isale Eko Market, before travelling to Tinubu market. Once I had finished at the markets, I finally went to Ebute Metta. Later that evening, I made my way to see Robert – the elation on his face was large. Robert had been the rock that prevented me from falling away into the bottomless pit of despair when I was so young, and I was glad to see him again. He was also thrilled to see me. We spoke for hours, and it was so late that I had to spend the night with Robert's family. They were all happy to accommodate me.

The following day, I attempted to locate Lemmy. I was told that he had moved to his village in Delta state to stay closer to his family. Nevertheless, I decided I would find another time to see him. I was upset that I couldn't see Lemmy. He had helped me get my first job and given me the opportunity to get away from the streets so many years ago. All I wanted was to greet him again and tell him I was doing okay. Two days later, I went to visit my dad, mainly to find out any information about Joy. When Tony got a sight of me, he moved towards me, touched my head and hugged me tenderly.

'Payoyo, is that you?'

'Yes papa.'

He hugged me tighter.

'Thank God you're alive and thank God you didn't forget home.'

I smiled; how could I ever forget home?

Everyone was surprised to see me, including Beki. She couldn't even look into my eyes; she simply gazed at the floor every time I tried to establish eye contact.

'Hi Beki,' I said.

'Hi.'

She walked away.

I didn't really expect much more from Beki; she must've been really uncomfortable seeing me. That aside, I met my half brothers and sisters: Vero, Larry, Tonia, Austin, Pala, Paul and Pauline. Vero and Larry still recognised me, but Tonia had only been a baby girl when I left home and Austin, Pala, Paul and Pauline were born while I was away. I felt like a stranger at Tony's home, but I didn't allow it to overcome my thoughts. I didn't visit Tony to remember the past. Tony was in a worse situation financially than when I'd left. He'd never recovered from the fire in 1978, but I wondered why he had seven children when he had no money to take care of them properly. I began to get carried away, criticising Tony's every decision, and I quickly tried to rid myself of those thoughts.

'Why am I here?' I constantly reminded myself.

Tony was getting older and was of little use to an employer. I couldn't bear the sight any longer.

'Papa, why did you have so many children when you're so poor?' I snidely remarked.

It was common for many households in Nigeria and perhaps across West Africa to believe that they had to have as many children as possible. Some families would often have more than twelve children, all born to a single woman. I just found it ridiculous that one woman could essentially give birth to an entire football team, with a few substitutes on the side.

Tony couldn't afford to have more children, yet he was taking no precautions to help himself. After he had remained silent for a long period of time, he replied.

'God gave me those children.'

Our discussion soon snowballed into an argument.

'Are you telling me I can't take care of my own children?'

'No. I'm telling you every child deserves to be looked after properly.'

Tony couldn't say a word. He looked into my face in search of an answer, but my stern answer continued to defy one. He had no money and we both knew it. Soon after our argument, Albert and his family heard that I was at Tony's place and came to see me. All of his children had grown up. I stayed with them all for a few hours.

Before I left, I promised to visit them again soon. Matthew, one of Albert's sons, accompanied me back to Mary's home. Once I arrived home with Matthew, Mary knew I had gone to see Tony. I thought she would be upset that I didn't speak to her about visiting Tony before I went. Conversely, she gave me a different response.

'I thought I'd have to force you before you paid Tony a visit,' she said. 'I'm glad you did.'

I narrated to Mary what happened at the visit, including my small argument with Tony. She also explained to me events that had happened since my departure. It was good to speak to Mary again after all that time.

'Come Peter, I've made your favourite dish.'

I was starving and couldn't wait to eat. There was silence on the dining table as we all ate. That's how we knew the meal was delicious. That night Matthew, Mary and I had a lot of fun and we didn't sleep until 4am the next morning. Home was great, but all of a sudden Gabon and Mama Cathy seemed a long way away.

Later in the evening, Mary wanted to know what I'd been through since I left to Gabon. She was always happy that I was alive, but upset that I hadn't made any real progress with regard to my education. We also spoke about Joy and how important it was for me to look for her. Ultimately, she was my sister and I felt obligated to find out where she was. While at Tony's place, I discovered that Joy had left for Kano, a Northern state of Nigeria. Mary presented me the first and only letter Joy ever sent, and thankfully there was an address at the top right corner of the page. At least I had a starting point.

After spending a week at Mary's home, I left for Vincent's home to prepare myself for the journey to Kano. I promised to see Mary before my return to Gabon; Matthew was also with me and we both left the village. Only a few hundred metres away from Vincent's home, I began having a terrible headache and decided to visit a pharmacy alongside the road. At the pharmacy, I met a girl. But as I stared, her face seemed familiar. And then I remembered that a week before, I had decided to take a bus from Tony's to Mary's home with Matthew. While crossing the overhead pedestrian bridge, I saw the same girl walking ahead of me. Her school bag fell to the ground, and her books and pencils spread out on the floor. We had helped pick up her belongings and she had thanked us.

'I remember you,' I said to her. 'Your bag fell on the floor and my friend and I helped you pick it up. We were on top of the overhead bridge in Mile 2.'

'I can't remember,' she nervously replied.

But her response proved to me that she did know; I just couldn't understand why she wouldn't accept it.

'But I remember you…Anyway, my name's Peter. What about you?'

'Rose.'

'Nice to meet you Rose. I have a really bad headache and need some Paracetamol.'

She gave me some Paracetamol and Matthew and I made our way to Vincent's home. Soon, I would be making my way to Kano.

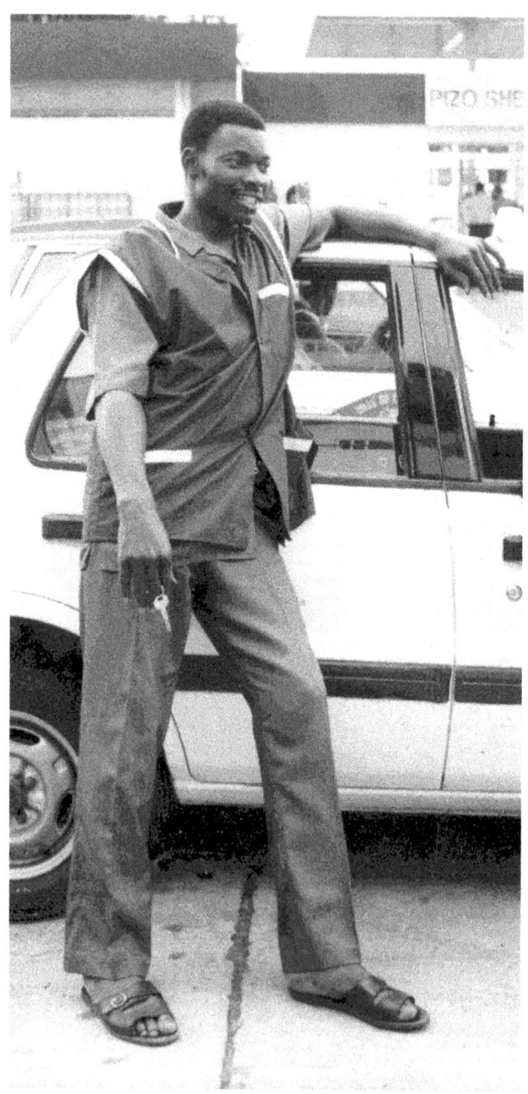

Eko and his taxi in Libreville

Me washing a car in Libreville

Me standing in front of the car wash

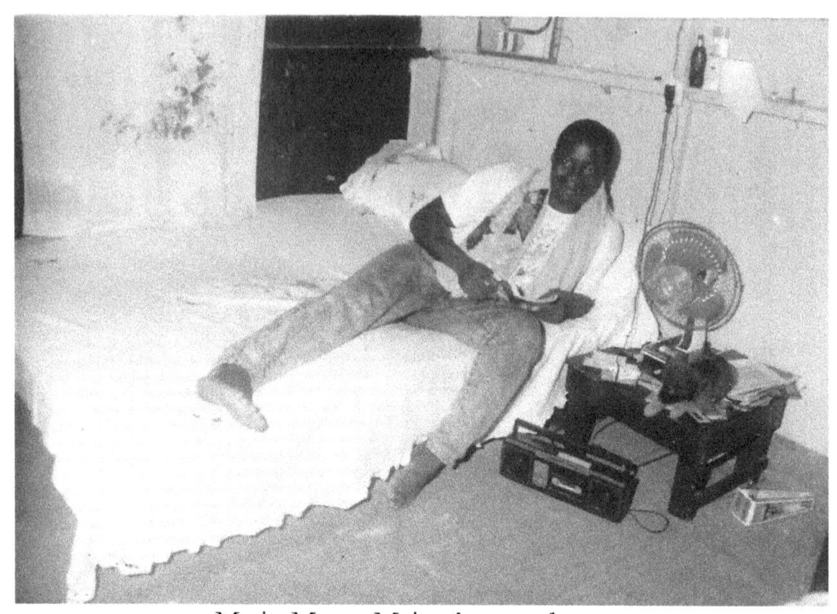

Me in Mama Maisey's rented room

Mama Cathy's mother, Ayito, (left) and I (right) in her room

Mama Cathy in her early adult years (left) and Hadija (right), Mama Cathy's relative

Feyisere (left), Keita (centre) and me (right) working at the block factory

Angwe (far left), Matthew (centre left), me (centre right) and Rotimi (far right) working at the block factory

Me at Briqueterie Ereb (the block factory)

Kouevi-Gath Akouete (left), Me (centre) and Jean-Bosco 'Jibé' (right)

M'bembi at eighteen years old in 1992

Tichou (left to right), Sulamite, M'bembi, Jonathan (front), Audrey, Benoni and Jibé

Me travelling from Leon M'ba Airport to Murtala Muhammad Airport

Chapter 11: A Little Trip to the North

Kano State is located in North-Western Nigeria and is the country's largest state. It is the second largest industrial centre, holds sector expert knowledge in pharmaceuticals, plastics and textiles, but is also home to the oldest continuous site of authority in Nigeria — the Emir's Palace. More than 600 miles away from Lagos, I would make the journey to Kano with my childhood friend Calis Emeka. I met Emeka on my last visit to Tony's home and he agreed to join me on my trip to Kano. It was a thirteen hour journey by car, but we were both looking forward to it. It would give us a lot of time to catch up with each other.

We decided to take public transport and left Vincent's home at about 4pm. Once we arrived in Oyingbo Motor Park, we got into a minibus with about sixteen passengers on board including myself. We spent a few hours in the motor park before it began to move. By this time, it was 6pm. We had been travelling for seven hours, when Emeka began tapping me on shoulder aggressively.

'Wake up Peter! Wake up!'

It was more the tumultuous screaming that awoke my enervated body. I couldn't hear myself in the cacophony of noise and looked outside the small windows to see what was going on. Almost touching, a lorry was driving alongside our vehicle. But the screaming was because somehow the lorry had attached itself to our minibus. We were travelling at speeds over 90 mph and heading straight for a large hole that would almost certainly crash the vehicle and send it into the sky somersaulting until it crashed violently into the ground and only the painful noise of metal cutting the ground would be heard. The driver began shouting.

'Everybody calm down!'

But no one was listening. People were trying to escape, but if they jumped, they would simply land in the road amidst the onrushing cars to the rear of us. There were only a few seconds left before we would hit the hole. I closed my eyes and said a prayer. Suddenly, the lorry driver swerved his vehicle to the right, jolting those of the minibus also to the right. We had managed to avoid the hole and finally amidst the chaos had detached ourselves from the minibus. The surge of relief that came over all of us was ineffable. We were mostly shaken, but without injuries. The driver pulled into the side of the road for everyone to calm down and tried to open the passenger door, but it wouldn't open. A few others tried to help the driver open the door, but to no avail. There were no mechanical garages nearby so the door would have to remain locked until we arrived at Kano.

Five hours later, we arrived at Kano Motor Park. I looked at the time; it was 7am. The door was forced open and we were let out. It was quite a remarkable experience. Emeka and I were both tired and although there was a small blip on our way to Kano, it was a pleasant and fun experience. Once we had gotten out of the bus, I looked at the letter that Mary had given us, which detailed Joy's address. I asked people around whether the address was nearby, but was told that Yellema was another three hour journey away.

Travelling on another bus, we made our way from the motor park to Yellema. When we got to Joy's address, we were told that she no longer lived in Yellema, but she was now living thirty minutes away in Hadejia, in a government residential area and worked as a nurse in one of the people's clinic. We had done so much travelling — almost 17 hours — and it had taken its toll on us.

Once we arrived at Hadejia's Motor Park, we were redirected to the people's clinic. As we advanced towards the clinic, I saw a person running towards us. As they got closer, I realised it was Joy.

'Joy!' I shouted.

'Peter!'

We embraced. I hadn't seen her for more than four years, and she had changed so much. It was incredible seeing Joy again; our happiness was evident to see.

In addition to the work she did at the people's clinic, Joy owned *Aunty Maggi's Restaurant* at Hadejia's main market, but was managed by a Ghanaian woman called Mama Ebenezer. Her restaurant was very nice and could accommodate about ten customers and local marketers loved having their lunch at Aunty Maggi's restaurant. I had never seen Joy so happy. I asked her why she never sent Mary another letter or at least sent a message back home to show she was still alive, but she simply replied.

'I'm just trying to move on from the past.'

We quickly moved away from that topic and made our way to the restaurant. Meanwhile, I was still recovering from my poorly condition from when I had left Mary's and it hadn't improved. I wasn't able to enjoy the meal because of it and Joy suggested that we make our way to her home. A few minutes later, I collapsed to the floor with fatigue. When I opened my eyes a few hours later, I saw that my arms were attached to intravenous drips and I was lying down on a bed in the clinic where Joy worked. I was really unwell; it took three days before I began regaining my strength and it wasn't until the fifth day that I felt fully well.

We hadn't been able to explain to each other how we were fairing because of my illness, but now we were able to talk. I explained everything that I had been through to Joy; from stowing away on the ship to the incident at Tony's place. When I had finished, Joy, with tears in her eyes, explained what happened since she left home.

'When you left, the home crumbled.'

She paused.

'After I graduated from secondary school, the situation at home worsened. Only a few days later, I got pregnant, but I decided to keep it a secret. I didn't know what to do; I couldn't handle the stress and eventually I had a miscarriage. But I knew I couldn't stay at home. So I decided to run away to the North.

Joy continued.

'I left home without informing anyone where I was going. Before I left for the North, I became a qualified nurse so I thought it would be easy to get a job at a clinic. At Yellema, where I used to stay, I met people who helped me find a nursing job at the people's clinic. Then, I found a place in Hadejia, which was closer to the clinic and so I moved there.

Joy had gone through a lot since I had left, but I was glad to see her well and surviving. Emeka and I had a lovely visit to Hadejia. Joy introduced me to most of her friends and colleagues. I asked if we could eat at her restaurant again, as the first time I wasn't able to enjoy my meal properly; this time, we had a fantastic time. Once we left the restaurant, Emeka and I had to make our way back to Lagos. I promised to visit her again soon and that was how I left Joy in Kano.

Late in the evening of the following day, I made my way to Mary's home and told her about Joy. She was so happy to hear that

Joy was well. I spent two more days at Mary's place, before I returned to Vincent's, from where I would return to Gabon. I said my last farewells to Mary and promised to visit her again.

When I arrived at Vincent's place, I began reflecting on my trip to Nigeria and I believed it to have been rather successful. I had managed to reunite with my family. I hadn't been able to locate Lemmy, but I did hand a letter to someone who knew him, hoping he would receive it. I had seen my friends and had a splendid time with Mary. What more could I have asked? It was a good break from Gabon, but now, it was time to return.

The following day, I boarded my flight back to Libreville. I didn't walk with the elegance I had when I first started my trip, instead, I was a refined man much akin with my thoughts. The novelty of boarding a plane had long worn off, now I was like everyone else – normal people going about their daily lives. I had work to get back to when I returned and what would happen between M'bembi and I was something I still needed to find out. For now though, I could sit and look out of the window at the clouds that danced gracefully in the blue skies. As I followed their movement, I was taken in a trance. My eyes got heavier and heavier. Then, when I could look no longer, I shut my eyes and slept.

Chapter 12: Dancing with Cupid

Arriving at Leon M'ba Airport, Mama Cathy and Eko were already waiting to welcome me back home.

'Mon enfant, welcome back,' Mama Cathy said, taking my bags from my hands.

I hugged her and Eko.

'Welcome back!' Eko added.

'Bonjour, bonjour! Thank you.'

We got into Eko's taxi.

'Eko, you need to paint this taxi again. The colour's fading.'

'Yes, I've actually been thinking about it. I shall do it soon.'

As usual, preceding everything she said, Mama Cathy added *mon enfant*, but she was doing it so regularly in simple sentences, it didn't seem normal.

'Mama Cathy, are you okay?' I asked.

'Yes, yes mon enfant. I'm just excited. God has sent you back to me.'

Eko and I laughed. What had gotten over her? Of course, I was coming back. It's not like there was anywhere else I could've gone, even if I wanted to. But I guess she was only happy to see me again and she had begun to miss me, I had missed her too. I'd missed going to the farm with her every Wednesday, and taking the mickey out of all my friends. The jokes we used to say were unbelievably funny and Mama Cathy's impersonations were always world class. But the repeated *mon enfant* had begun to make me a little uncomfortable.

We arrived home relatively quickly, but nothing could have prepared me for what I was about to see. After my bath, I made my way to the dining table to eat. After having sat down and washed my hands in the bowl of water in front of me, I began salivating over the smell of food from the kitchen.

'When is the food coming over?'

'Mon enfant, be patient, be patient.'

As I stood up to see what was happening in the kitchen and assist Mama Cathy in bringing the food to the table, I was surprised to see Jessica carrying my food to the dining table. I then intently marched to the kitchen.

'What is this about?' I asked angrily. 'Can you please explain to me what Jessica is doing here?'

She tried to think of an answer.

'Mon enfant…'

But no words could come out of her mouth.

'Don't *mon enfant* me. Just tell me what Jessica is doing here Mama Cathy. I would like to know.'

I could sense the apprehension in Mama Cathy; Jessica was standing behind us and watching events unfold in the kitchen.

'Jessica has been helping me since you left to Nigeria. She is my guest, not yours. So leave the poor girl alone.'

'Fine, but if she's your guest you must serve her, or she can serve you. But she won't serve me.'

Mama Cathy walked away from me. I knew she was unhappy with my behaviour, but what she had done was unfair. She didn't tell me that Jessica was here. I had just returned from Nigeria and on the day I return, this is what I'm faced with. If you take a donkey to the stream to drink water, can you force the donkey to drink water? No. So even if I was the child who didn't know how to look after himself, I would not be forced, on any condition, to marry a person I did not love. If I wasn't as hungry as I was, I would have just left the room, but I was starving. I served myself and began to eat. I refrained from conversing with Mama Cathy and Jessica at the table. As soon as I finished eating, I made my way to my bed. It was good to be home, but equally it wasn't great kick-starting my return with the Jessica matter. I thought that had ended months ago…Clearly, I was wrong.

The following morning, I heard someone knocking on my door.

'Who is it?' I asked.

'It's me, mon enfant,' Mama Cathy said. 'I want to speak to you.'

'Come in, the door isn't locked.'

Mama Cathy walked in.

'I'm sorry about last night. Perhaps it was the wrong time for Jessica to visit.'

'The wrong time? I told you that I've never liked Jessica and yet you force her upon me.'

'What can I do? I've seen you with no other woman and when I bring you Jessica you say no. You're starting to make me think something else.'

'I'm fine Mama Cathy. I just don't like Jessica.'

'You're not fine at all. You need to get married. You just can't continue like this.'

'Okay Mama Cathy. I've heard you.'

'You've heard me?'

'Yes.'

'You better act on it Peter,' Mama Cathy said as she left the room. 'Or else I will act for you. And even if you don't marry Jessica, you'd better find someone now and fast, because I will not wait for you.'

With that she left the room. I knew my time was now limited. If Mama Cathy acted, that would be it — literally. I needed an urgent solution to this problem. A week later, I went back to work at the block factory. Getting back into education was now a distant memory; I simply had no time. The amount of time I spent at the block factory proved how addicted I had become to my work. The block factory was growing from strength to strength and with the help of Olga, the managing director of *Entreprise de Réfection et Entretien Bâtiment*, a building contractors' company, my sales were increasing dramatically. She would help me secure building block orders. With the amount of money being generated, I decided to build a mini restaurant and bar, especially for the block moulders, who would sometimes spend longer than eighteen hours working at the factory. A few months later, it turned into a fully-fledged evening restaurant and bar, and gradually became popular in the area. During this time, Mama Cathy introduced me into her religion and taught me a lot of things about her rite. Soon afterwards, I devoted myself to the faith.

Concentrating on my work so much I hadn't realised how quickly time had flown by. I was now twenty three years old, and still without a wife. It had been some time since my conversation with Mama Cathy, and I began dreading the worst. Although I began to become more interested in other girls, M'bembi still held my heart and as far as I knew, we were still in a relationship. I'd seen her twice since my return from Lagos, and wished I could see her more often. But I couldn't; Jean was only ever away from his daughter for a few seconds, nothing more. I was incredibly worried about her and hoped her father hadn't been too harsh. I went to see Jibé and asked if he had any information about M'bembi. His words confirmed to me what I had suspected. Jean was restricting his daughter's freedom and was threatening to send her back to Zaire. She had been warned never to speak to me or set her eyes on me ever again. What would happen to our relationship? My concern grew, but Jibé said he would find a way for M'bembi and me to meet. Two days after our conversation, I received a letter from M'bembi.

Mon Amour,

I'm deeply sorry that I've been unable to write or see you. I know you'll be worried. My father has become a fervent obstacle to our relationship. I've thought about running away or getting a baby with you, but I know you won't allow it.

Wherever I go, he follows me. I have no freedom — nothing. Things are getting out of hand. And although it kills me not to be with you, I don't think our relationship can work. Please do me a small favour and marry Jessica. I know Mama Cathy wants you to marry her. And my father has vowed he will never allow a Nigerian to marry his daughter... But I will try, we will try.

Peter, this is it. Please go, for my heart is troubled and aching. We will meet at a later time. But as for my father, he will live to regret his actions.

I love you, and always will.

M'bembi.

After reading the letter, I was deeply upset, but thought it was better to stay apart for the moment. Jessica continued to visit Mama Cathy's home, and Mama Cathy wouldn't relent with her pressure. It was so tense at home that I spent most of my time at work, just to get away from Mama Cathy. There were simply too many problems at hand, and so I decided I needed something purposeful and distracting to do that wasn't work.

I loved keeping fit and my favourite sport at the time was weightlifting. We didn't have any weightlifting discs and so I used cement as my weights. I would mix gravel, sand, cement and water and pour it into different sized bowls for it to set. They would form large sphere-shaped stones and I would vary the weights of each stone I made. I soon created a mini training ground near the block factory. Residents in the local area would visit the training ground and attempt to carry some of the weights. It was an enjoyable period and it kept me away from home and Mama Cathy's constant reminders.

After having only spent a few weeks in Gabon, I was thinking about returning to Nigeria and visiting Mary. Sooner than I had realised, I found myself in Lagos once more. The aim of the visit this time was to meet a few old friends, get a break from Mama Cathy (though I never told her that) and mend my relationship with Tony. I firstly went to Albert's home to take Matthew in company, before I stopped at Tony's home. Compared to my previous visit, there was a level of calmness I hadn't seen before that hit me as I entered Tony's home. Yet, this serenity only deceived people from the adversity my father faced financially and physically. Proving my words correct from my last visit, the family wasn't doing very well. As I began thinking about how I could help, Tony asked me a question.

'I was wondering whether you could take one of your sisters abroad with you.'

My father had finally realised that he couldn't take care of all his children. I was quiet; I didn't really know how to respond.

Should I say 'I told you so' and weaken our relationship further or accept his desperate request? After a few minutes, I responded.

'Okay, give me time to think about it.'

He didn't reply.

'You haven't asked how I'm keeping abroad or about my education.'

The silence in between our replies was sharp and piercing.

'What do you want me to say?' he replied slowly. 'I know a lot of things have gone wrong, but I've decided to place the past behind me.'

Before I left Tony's place, I was curious to find out who he intended for me to take abroad.

'Who's the person you want me to take?' I asked.

I could sense a slight glimmer in his heart.

'Tonia.'

Tonia had just finished primary school and was eleven years old. She was only a young girl, but I needed to think deeply about taking her. I was still trying to build my business in Gabon. I guess the habit that traditional African parents have to pass parental responsibilities on their capable children was what I was experiencing. The intergenerational poverty that affected Tony was now being passed to me. If he couldn't handle his misfortunes, he'd pass it on to his child — just like the rest of them.

Instead of trying to get out of their problem, traditional African parents have the tendency to bury their heads in the sand. But when they see that one Pelé or Maradona out of their lack-lustre football team, they ask him to carry them through — coach and everyone. I always admired the German football team; they were efficient, meticulous and left nothing to chance. The manager had a long term plan and built towards his goal. If only African parents built their home like the Germans build their team. If only they did not allow poverty to consume them and think social mobility was impossible. If only when they had children they thought of it as a long-term project.

Tony had eleven children in total; one with a woman he later left, three with Elizabeth and seven with Beki. Imagine if he had had two to four children. Perhaps he would have cared for them better. Perhaps if he thought about the long term, he would have cared for all eleven of his children better. But the past cannot be changed, when it has already been written; I just hope it is not rewritten for families to come.

Later that afternoon, Matthew and I made our way to Vincent's home. I promised to visit Tony before I departed for Gabon. Beki was always nearby to Tony whenever I spoke to him, but she would never say a word. Always quiet. But before I arrived at Vincent's quarters, I stopped at the pharmacy where I met Rose, the day I had a painful headache. However, on this occasion, I met a young man called Nicolas.

'Hello my friend, how are you?'

'I'm fine thank you. How can I help sir?'

'I was just wondering where Rose is.'

'Rose? I don't know who Rose is sir. Perhaps you are at the wrong place.'

I turned to Matthew.

'Is this not the chemist where we met Rose that day?'

'Yes, this is the chemist.'

'We met a young girl here when we came,' I said looking at Nicolas.

'We don't have a Rose here. Maybe you're thinking of Samantha.'

'No, she said her name was Rose. The woman here.'

I then described to Nicolas how Rose looked.

'That fits the description of Samantha,' Nicolas replied. 'She's the daughter of the pharmacy's owner.'

I left a message for Samantha with Nicolas and soon afterwards, Matthew and I made our way to Vincent's home.

The following day, while I was at the back of Vincent's quarters, I saw a person who appeared to look like Samantha through a gap in the fence.

'Rose! Rose!' I shouted.

I received no reply.

'Samantha!'

She turned around and I was able to get a good look at her face.

'So your name's not Rose,' I said to myself silently.

I slid through the gap in the fence and began calling her.

'Stop! I want to talk with you.'

My plea fell on deaf ears; she didn't even turn around. She just kept on walking and at a fast pace. I ran in front of her.

'Hey! What are you doing?' she shouted.

'It's me, Peter, we met a few months ago.'

'What? Leave me alone. I don't know who you are!'

Instantly, I stopped trying to speak to her in fear I had mistaken her for someone else. I watched her walk off into the distance, with myself a little embarrassed. As I went back inside, I couldn't help to think that that was Samantha.

'She turned her head when I called her name,' I thought. 'How could it not be her?'

I couldn't to get a grip of myself. I decided to head back to the chemist and speak with Nicolas.

'Nicolas I saw her.'

'Saw who.'

'Rose. Samantha. That girl I was talking to you about yesterday.'

'Oh yeah, Samantha. What about her?'

'I saw her in the road. I called her Rose, but she didn't respond. Then I called Samantha and she turned around. I tried to speak with her, but she shouted at me.'

Nicolas started laughing. I couldn't see what was so funny.

'Come with me,' he said. 'I'll help you.'

Nicolas worked for Samantha's mother. Samantha's mother was known as 'Mama Nurse' and Samantha was known as 'Ọmọ Mama Nurse'; *Ọmọ* being Yoruba for child. Nicolas and Samantha lived in the same building and so he escorted me to their home.

'Stay here. I'll be back.'

I stood outside their home for a few minutes before I saw Samantha come to the door.

'You again! What do you want from me?'

She didn't want to talk to me.

'So you're Samantha, not Rose. Why did you lie to me?' I asked.

'Nicolas must've told you my name, but the reason I told you my name was Rose was because I didn't want boys coming to disturb me. And my mother doesn't tolerate it.'

I wasn't completely sure if I knew what I was doing, but I thought I needed a girlfriend, especially since my relationship with M'bembi was tentative. I looked at this as an opportunity. Quickly, Samantha and I became friends once we got to know each other; though it wasn't what I'd describe as a relationship. A few days after my visit to Samantha's home, I met Nuru, Samantha's brother and Kikẹ, Samantha's sister. I became very close friends with Nuru; it was a great friendship. Slowly but surely, I was getting closer to Samantha.

Meanwhile, Mama Cathy was unyielding with her phone calls. Because she didn't know the date I was coming back, near every day, she would ask when I was returning to Gabon. I didn't have much time left in Nigeria and so I visited Mary's home, as promised. I spent a few days with her, before I left. After spending more than a month in Nigeria, I felt it was time to leave. Sadly, I was unable to locate Lemmy or keep my promise to Tony. I was also so wrapped up in trying to develop a relationship with Samantha that I nearly forgot about returning back to Gabon. Hoping to see everyone soon, I boarded my flight back to Libreville.

As I sat in the plane, I began to think about my relationship with M'bembi and Samantha. What was I doing? Could you love two people at the same time? Since Jean's opposition to the relationship between M'bembi and me, I'd been distracted with other women. Perhaps I was desperate or lovesick. I really liked Samantha and our relationship was growing, but I also liked M'bembi. Yet with M'bembi, there seemed like no solution. I couldn't figure out what I wanted to do.

What would you have done?

Chapter 13: Feeling Sick

I was glad to be back home in Libreville. Mama Cathy desperately wanted me to marry Jessica. I couldn't recall the numerous times that I had told Mama Cathy that I didn't want to marry her. But she wouldn't have it. She couldn't go an entire day without talking about Jessica. Sometimes, she would invite her home and I'd wait until late at night to return when I found out she had come. I didn't know what to do. I'd been blunt, forthright, given the same message consistently and yet, I was still faced with the same problem.

A few months later, I couldn't understand why, but my love for M'bembi grew again. I decided I would take one last chance with M'bembi. I really wanted to find out if M'bembi's father was truly being serious that he would not allow me to marry his daughter because I was Nigerian. I spoke to Jibé about accompanying me on a visit to M'bembi's father and he agreed. I knew if I spoke with M'bembi, she'd prevent me from seeing her father. But I just wanted to see if Jean could perhaps have a change of heart if he saw how sincere I was towards his daughter. I rehearsed what to say and how to say it. I even said it aloud to Jibé, but no matter how prepared I tried to be, I was still nervous. How would Jean react?

Two weeks later, Jibé and I visited M'bembi's father. When we arrived, we were told to sit in front of his mechanic's workshop; Jean was a car mechanic and he was busy repairing a customer's vehicle. A few minutes later, he came out from his workshop and was greatly surprised to see Jibé and me. Before Jean could speak, Jibé spoke.

'Peter is here to see you and I have come with him.'

There was a pause. Jibé jumped in again.

'Peter has come to receive approval. Please give your approval to M'bembi's and Peter's relationship. Peter loves your daughter and M'bembi loves him too. Even you have witnessed it. I beg you to accept Peter.'

Hearing Jibé's word, I unquestionably knew that my chances were blown. Jean hadn't even starting speaking, but his eyes told the whole story.

'I have told you to stay away from my daughter! Look, I'm busy. I don't want to discuss this issue with you again.'

Sadly, the visit didn't go as I had planned. We hurriedly left his workshop so as not to provoke him any further. I just hoped nothing would happen to M'bembi because of the step I had taken.

It was difficult to see M'bembi, but a few days later, Jibé managed to plan a meeting for me to meet M'bembi at Mama Sophie's home. After making sure that no one was following me, I made my way into Mama Sophie's home, and sitting down on her sofa I saw M'bembi. As soon as she saw, we both jumped into our arms and embraced.

'I heard what happened at the workshop with my father,' she said pitifully. 'I'm so sorry. My mother tried to stick up for you, but he just fought her. It was frightening. Things are not going well.'

At hearing this, I became overwhelmed. I didn't want to be the cause of the collapse of Jean's relationship with his wife.

'What are we going to do?' I asked.

'I love you Peter and I've promised not to marry anyone else, but…'

'We can do something about it. I'm sure of it. We could run away…'

'No…I don't want my father to hurt you. I don't want any of us to get hurt…'

Her pause concerned me.

'Let's just end this.'

'What?'

'The relationship.'

'You're joking me,' I said, puzzled. 'You can't be serious?'

'I love you Peter…'

'I love you too…'

'But, and let me finish,' she said. 'We can't be together. Don't make this any harder for me.'

She began to cry. I held her tighter. She then whispered in my ear, almost as if someone was watching us.

'My father will regret this.'

The defiance and menacing intent in her last five words were sharp. She unwrapped herself from within my warm coil.

'But I love you M'bembi. Please. Give us another chance.'

She began to weep heavily, resisting me from holding her hands.

'Peter, go!'

I was stunned into silence; I stopped. I looked into her face in search for the girl I fell in love with. But I didn't see it. Instead, her young eyes were tired like a man who had witnessed murders beyond imagination. The water that flooded her eyes had drowned the burning radiance she once had. There was nothing I could do. No words would have changed her mind. But at that moment I noticed it wasn't the same M'bembi I knew. These words were not her own. With my head down to the ground, in disbelief, I left Mama Sophie's house. Before I left, Mama Sophie spoke softly in my ear.

'I wish she was my daughter. Take heart.'

I was distraught. Heartbroken beyond repair, I didn't know what to do with myself. After all the moments we'd shared and how much we loved each other, we could no longer be together. My first ever love, my first ever relationship destroyed by a man who simply did not like Nigerians. I couldn't bring myself to terms with the loss. It was like someone taking your most valuable piece of china, perhaps the most historic and precious in the world, and cynically hurling it to the ground where it instantly shattered into a tiny million pieces. And then when you asked them why they did it, they said 'I just don't like it'.

In the following days, my depression and regret grew. I was lovesick. I couldn't eat or sleep. I didn't go to work and just lay on the bed in my room. Even Mama Cathy began to ask why I was feeling so low. Slowly, Jessica's visits lessened and she wouldn't talk to me about Jessica. Jibé continued to console and strengthen me. He was a good friend to me; I appreciated that. I still loved M'bembi greatly.

It had been too long since I'd seen Texan and really wanted to see him again. I had received no news from him and wondered if he was okay. I approached the farm driver who had taken him to the next village and asked if he had seen Texan recently, but the farm driver said he hadn't. At that point, I decided to go to the village myself. I needed to get away from the home anyway and give myself some breathing space. Once I arrived at the village, I was told that no one had seen him for more than seven months; he had just vanished. Surprised, I wrote a letter and asked Texan's neighbour to give it to him when he returns.

More and more frequently, I was receiving messages from Tony asking me to help him look after my half-sister, Tonia. I was wrapped up in so many things I couldn't concentrate. I had to cope with work, losing M'bembi and now caring for my half-sister. I thought about ignoring it, but I couldn't. I had found out that most of my half brothers and sisters had dropped out of school because of finances. I didn't want them to experience the same problem with education I had, so I spoke to Mama Cathy about taking in Tonia. She was quite happy with it and we agreed it would be fine. Tonia had finished primary school so perhaps staying with me would help her refocus on her education. Once Mama Cathy and I had thought of a plan, we sent a letter to Tony about the necessary arrangements. Meanwhile, I was also planning a trip to Nigeria. Perhaps that would give me a break away from the troubles of Gabon. A few weeks later, I found myself in Murtala Muhammed International Airport.

Chapter 14: November 1994

I had been sitting in the Airport for over an hour, and yet he had still not arrived. Although I guess some blame rests on me for not planning my pick up, he was always there. Instead, I had to get 1020's friends, Niyi, to take me to Vincent's home. We soon arrived at Vincent's home. I left my bags in the car with Niyi while I went to knock for Vincent so he'd open the gate.

'Hello.'

'Good afternoon.'

'You must be Vincent's brother?'

'Yes. Is he in there?

'Hi, I'm Binta. I'm a friend to Vincent's fiancé,' she continued. 'Vincent has moved. This is his new address.'

She gave me a piece of paper.

'Thank you... How did you know who I was?'

'Oh, I saw you in one of his pictures.'

'Oh right, okay. It was nice meeting you Binta. See ya.'

'Yeah, same here. Bye.'

The gate closed and I went back to the taxi.

'My brother's moved. Take me to this address,' I said as I passed the piece of paper to Niyi.

It was less than a thirty minute drive to Vincent's new place. He told me that his old address was where I would be lodging into whenever I wanted to visit Nigeria and that he had especially reserved a place for me. I was incredibly grateful to my brother.

A couple of days later, I visited Tony's home. I needed to be quick with my planning as I only had a little amount of time to sort things out, which included taking Tonia and me back to Gabon. Unfortunately, Tonia couldn't accompany me to Gabon because there was limited space available on the airline. As a result, she had to make the trip in the supervision of one of my friends, Bisi. Tonia would soon be departing from Murtala Muhammed International Airport with Air Gabon. I was excited to see her travelling on a plane. Tonia was elated, but Beki didn't look so happy. I began to wonder if she was really happy with the situation. Nevertheless, all the arrangements had been made and Tonia was travelling to Gabon. I simply hoped her journey would happen smoothly.

It soon got dark and I had to be travelling home. Matthew was always with me when I came to Nigeria and was a great aid to me. He was my right hand man per se, and was also a very good friend. That night, most of the food outlets had closed, including the restaurants; we were very hungry and needed something to eat, but all our efforts were futile so we headed home. On our way back, however, we met Samantha. She was surprised to see me.

'Hi Peter! When did you arrive?'

'Just a few days ago,' I replied.

Matthew and I were starving. I continued.

'We were just looking for food…'

Matthew cut in.

'It's so difficult to find any place to eat around here.'

'Are you guys hungry then?'

'Yes, very,' I replied.

'Okay then. Peter, you can go home. Matthew, you come with me.'

At that, Matthew left me. Why would she tell me to go home? I was hungrier than Matthew and he was five years younger than me.

'Look after the elderly first,' I thought.

Forty minutes later, Matthew returned. In his hands, he carried white, fluffy cooked rice, with stew and a large mackerel fish placed on top like a cherry on a cake. The smell was compelling. I told Matthew to place it on the table while I washed my hands. I sat comfortably on my seat and began eating. With sweat protruding from my forehead, it would seem like I had just run the 10,000 metres in an Olympic final. Halfway through the meal, I noticed Matthew staring at me. Hadn't he eaten at Samantha's?

'Hey Matthew, why are you looking at me like that?'

'I'm hungry.'

'Didn't you eat at Samantha's?

'No, I just brought the food.'

Realising what I had just done, I quickly apologised to Matthew. I couldn't believe that I had had half of the meal right in front of him. Imagine what he'd be thinking about me.

'Matthew, you can have the rest.'

As soon as Matthew was about to take the plate from my hands, Samantha walked in. Finding out what happened, she asked Matthew to go with her. A few minutes later, Matthew came in with another full plate of cooked rice. And that smelt even better than the first one. Biting my bottom lip, the desire to take some of Matthew's food was overwhelming. But I couldn't allow myself. That was Matthew's plateful.

Samantha and I got even closer than we were during my stay in Lagos. I spent most of my time with her, and as the days passed, I began to fall in love with her.

A week later, Tonia departed for Libreville. But soon after, I became very ill. I was so ill that I missed my flight; I just couldn't get on the plane. It took about two weeks for me to recover from my fever. Soon after I recovered, I went to see Mary in the village, accompanied by Samantha. Mary was happy to see me and Samantha. In private, Mary began to ask me a few questions.

'Peter, who is she?'

'She's my friend.'

'Friend? Do you like her?'

'Yes.'

'Well I suggest you move quickly because she is a very nice girl.'

Mary encouraged me to marry Samantha. The only problem was I didn't want to create another Jessica situation, but reversed. And I wasn't too sure about committing myself to another relationship, especially after M'bembi. Following our visit, Samantha and I both returned our separate ways home. A few hours later, I heard a knock on my door. I wondered who it might be, especially at 8pm. Opening the door, I found Samantha.

'Samantha! What are you doing here?'

Looking into my eyes, and holding my hands, she spoke.

'I love you Peter.'

I couldn't explain it. Perhaps it was libido, but it just came out of the blue. She'd always tell me she couldn't stay out longer than 7pm because of her parents, and now she'd come to me at 8pm and told me she loved me. I didn't want anything I would regret to happen that night. My creed had taught me how to remain chaste until marriage. Lifting her hands off me, I asked her a question.

'Do you really love me?'

'Yes and I'll do anything to prove it.'

'I was denied the love of my heart, and I don't know if I'm ready to get into another relationship.'

Over my young age, I had learned that parents could be obstacles to relationships. I always thought that your parents should love the person you love as if it were their own child. Yet, the behaviour of Jean proved that perhaps I was being naïve. Some parents tell you the person you love is a terrible human and not worthy of your love. They give you their own preference, but you don't love them. Then you go through a plethora of relationships and each time you say you love a new person, they say you're blinded or don't know what you want, and they never relent until you love someone who fits their preference. This thought ran around my head again and again and again.

'She said she'd do anything for me,' I thought.

'Will you marry me?'

I was completely and utterly crazy. A few moments ago, I'd just told her that I wasn't ready and now I was asking her to marry me.

'Yes, I will.'

It all happened so quickly. Before 8pm on the day I visited my mother, I was not engaged. Now all of sudden, I am.

'If you truly love me, prove it.'

What was I saying? Was I going too fast? Was I rushing?

'Come and see my parents and we'll get married straight away.'

What was I doing? Honestly…

A few days passed, and we arranged to see Samantha's parents. I sent two people to represent me. After my experience with Jean, I knew I would be too apprehensive to give off a good impression, especially since I was told that Samantha's parents were also very strict. A few hours later, I received the report of the visit.

'Should I tell you the good news or the bad news first?

'I don't know. Just tell me what happened.'

'They'll let you marry her.'

As I was about to hug Samantha, the bad news followed.

'They don't want her to get married now. They want you to wait.'

Samantha's parents approved of our relationship, but refused to approve the marriage, saying that Samantha was still too young. After that, I also began to think about the implications of marriage. I firmly guided my life on the religious principle of remaining chaste till after marriage. Yet, if I got married, I would not have respected this principle, and my faith thoroughly disagreed with engaging in such conduct outside marriage. Jibé was always telling me how he couldn't wait to marry his fiancé and have children. I also knew the penalties that came with this. It was something we were obligated to obey as religious people. Yet, there I was, *contemplating* the decision.

Additionally, my creed also encouraged that we married people in the faith, and Samantha wasn't in my faith. M'bembi was part of the same religion and so was Jessica, so I'd never really faced that dilemma before. But it was obvious that I wanted to marry Samantha. Perhaps it was an escape from Jessica, or I was recovering from my lovesickness, but I wanted to marry her.

Nights after nights passed and yet Samantha and I remained chaste. It was extremely difficult and the temptation began to grow as the nights went. About two weeks after we received news about our marriage from Samantha's parents, Samantha asked me a question.

'Do you really love me?'

'Of course I love you. Would I be marrying you if I didn't? I said — the question almost rhetorical to myself.

'Then let's leave my parents out of this.'

'What do you suggest?'

'We want to get married right?'

'Yes.'

'Then let's get married.'

'What about your parents?'

Then what Samantha said hit me.

'You want us to get married without your parents knowing?'

I paused, while she looked at me.

'Let's do it then.'

It was perhaps the toughest decision of my life. But a few days later, on the 23rd November 1994, at twenty four years old, Samantha and I got married. Without the knowledge of Samantha's parents, we wed at a local registry. That night we pleased our curiosity; I was no longer celibate. I'm glad I respected my faith's principles, but I knew once they found out about it there would be a few things to discuss. To say we knew each other perfectly well could not be said, but we loved each other and we thought we could overcome any problems that would come our way. Perhaps that was good enough. Perhaps it wasn't, but for now, we would keep it a secret. Causing unnecessary hullabaloo would create an abundance of stress for us both and we didn't really want it.

My time in Nigeria was gradually coming to an end and my return to Gabon was imminent. Tonia had been in Gabon without me for just over a month and I needed to join her soon. A few days after our legal marriage, I left Samantha in Nigeria, but promised to be back soon. I thought about taking her with me to Gabon, but we'd have to see how things went.

I knew when I returned Mama Cathy would continue trying to make me marry Jessica, but I was already married to Samantha. In disbelief myself, I shook my head and smiled.

Chapter 15: A Bottle of Schnapps

Mama Cathy was furious.

'What's wrong mama?' I asked.

Never had I seen Mama Cathy so angry before. Incandescent and displeased, I was reproached like a small child.

'What's wrong mama?' I asked again, trying to find out what I had done wrong.

'What's wrong? What's *wrong*? Why did you send your younger sister without accompanying her?' she calmly replied.

Hearing that, I became afraid at what Tonia may have done to offend Mama Cathy. Frankly, Mama Cathy was rarely ever that angry.

'Where is Tonia?' I hurriedly asked.

'How am I meant to know? That is *your* responsibility. All I know is that since three weeks ago she hardly stays home.'

'Tonia doesn't stay at home?' I asked myself.

I hadn't spent more than five minutes back home and here I was being scolded by Mama Cathy, while being told that Tonia is somewhere gadding across Gabon. But the question that perhaps bothered me the most was why Tonia was not staying at home and where she was going. Completely unhappy, I waited for Tonia to arrive home.

It was about 11.30pm and Tonia had still not returned. Mama Cathy had gone to bed, while I sat in the living room. As I began to get irritable, I heard the door slowly creak open; it was Tonia.

'Where are you coming from?'

Tonia jumped. Astounded at seeing me, she remained silent, almost dumbfounded.

'Didn't you hear me?'

She was refusing to answer my questions and my irritation levels were slowly rising.

'Why have you acted this way?' I asked. 'Can you please explain to me what went wrong?'

I stood up to approach her, but my patience was thinning. Her silence was intolerable and in a burst of anger I yelled.

'TALK TO ME!'

I stopped, as the room fell silent.

'I want to return to Nigeria,' she replied calmly, unshaken by my yelling.

'You want to do what?' I responded, utterly shocked by her response.

'I want to return to Nigeria,' she repeated.

'But why? What has gotten into you?'

She didn't answer. She just continued to look at me in silence. I couldn't explain it. This wasn't the girl who was so elated to be travelling to Gabon I once saw, and I was shocked.

'Has anyone offended you? Has Mama Cathy done anything wrong to you while I was away?'

'I just don't like it here. I want to return to Lagos.'

As soon as I was to ask her why she wanted to return to Lagos, she reached for her pocket and brought out a letter.

'This is for you,' she said.

The letter was from the Nigerian Embassy in Gabon and asking me to visit the Nigerian Embassy immediately upon my return from Nigeria. After reading the contents of the letter, I sent Tonia to bed. Tomorrow was going to be a long day.

The following day, and early in the morning, I made my way to the Nigerian Embassy. I was not a stranger and most of them had recognised me from my last visit. Upon speaking with the officials at the Embassy, I was advised to take Tonia back to Lagos as soon as possible, but nobody, not even Tonia could answer me why. Tonia's silence over her reason began to frustrate the immigration officers, including Mr Miniru.

'Take her back with the next available flight, or else she'll run away.'

It just didn't make any sense to me. The whole point why Tonia had come to Libreville was to get a better education and for me to take care of her. But now I was being asked to take her back to Nigeria, but acquiring ticket money was not cheap! Then again, the consequence of not taking her back would be great. What could I do?

I tried to dissuade Tonia from leaving, but all my efforts were futile. She had made up her mind and it was not changing. She wanted to leave Libreville immediately. She wouldn't consider my opinion, the stress I would go through or the decision to bring her to Libreville in the first place. Then I began to question myself: was it because I didn't accompany her like Mama Cathy said? Was it my late return? But there was nothing I could say to Tonia to make her change her mind; not even a thousand tears.

Mama Cathy was also unhappy and bitterly complained.

'I don't know what happened to her,' she continued. 'Mama Juju is encouraging Tonia to make this decision. Sometimes, Tonia will spend more than three days at her place.'

I was completely surprised to hear this. Mama Juju was Papa Juju's wife and we were very good friends. I'd be shocked if they were encouraging Tonia and so I visited Mama Juju.

'If it wasn't for my advice and me keeping her in my home, Tonia would have run away,' she told me.

Tonia's stay with me was turning messy; I just had to figure out a way to let Tonia leave. I didn't have much money on me. I'd spent most of it on my trip to Nigeria. So it would take me at least a good month or two for me to raise enough money to buy plane tickets. Moreover, for a visa to be issued, it would take a minimum of two weeks, and that's if they were being nice. I realised that I had to find an alternative way to take Tonia back home.

A few days after my trip to the embassy, I met Tom. He introduced me to another route to Nigeria, a route that cost a considerably lesser amount of money, but one of which held a lot of risk. But there was nothing I could do; there was no choice. That night, Tom visited me.

'We will be departing from Ponoma. When the time gets closer, I will tell you.'

Ponoma was an area of commercial activity and hardly a place you dreamed of living in. Trades were happening all the time, especially with fresh fish from the water. A lot of foreigners came to Ponoma, but most never returned. Homes were built too close to the sea so that the tide would sweep under the beams that the house was built upon and cause them to shake. The air was thick and smoggy, the area was run-down, and the fumes of smoke that came from the roasted fish gave it the look of an industrial wasteland. But beneath this, Ponoma was amongst the three main human smuggling hubs in Gabon: Coco beach, Pubel and Ponoma. People risked their lives to migrate to another country by sea. Some would make it, but others would not. News came nearly every month of how people were either arrested by maritime police, or how boats sank in the sea, or how the bodies of women and young children were lost in the ocean. The stories that came back should have deterred people to take the trip, yet people were prepared to risk their lives to escape poverty in their country.

Tom instructed me carefully on what I had to do and the risks associated with the journey. He warned me not to disclose any information about the journey to Mama Cathy, but he didn't want me to take the trip. He asked to take Tonia himself so that I would stay in Gabon, but I couldn't do it. I'd not kept my eye on her once and I wasn't going to make the same mistake twice. I had stowed away on a ship before, so I thought I had some experience. But the route we were taking was unfamiliar to me and so I would have to draw on Tom's experience, especially as he had navigated the route many times before.

It'd been three days since Tom's last visit and our preparation had been meticulous. We had to travel in the quiet hours of the night so as not to get noticed. At about midnight, Tom visited us. We were to be taken to Ponoma. When we arrived, we saw men, women and young children. Twenty of us were instructed to get into a small boat and lay low face-down. We weren't to say a word to each other, until we were instructed further on what we had to do. The driver of the boat then moved across the water slowly till he stopped. To avoid detection by the maritime police, we didn't move for several hours. Once the driver saw there were no maritime police nearby, we were allowed to sit down.

We travelled for several hours by sea in the open boat. We were hit by the rain, scorched by the sun, violated by the waves and threatened by sharks. The paranoia that came over you in the dark was a harrowing, frightening experience. But urinating and defecating wasn't a real problem if you were happy to lose a little dignity. To defecate we had to place our rears on the edge of the boat and dump in the sea — so much for privacy.

We were moving along the water, slowly but quietly until suddenly one of our engines stopped. Ahead of us there was a large fish, perhaps a whale and it was heading straight for us. The driver turned off the second engine, apprehensive of what was heading straight for us. We thought we were going to be capsized. The fish, only about ten seconds away from the boat, went underwater. Everyone in the boat began turning their heads, looking in the water, some began to stand, some almost ready to jump. My eyes were shifting from left to right as I held Tonia close to me. Minutes passed and nothing happened. The captain signalled to the driver to turn the working engine back on; we were on the move again.

It took over two days to fix the engine that stopped working on the boat. Instead of arriving in Nigeria in four to five days, we had now spent ten days on the sea. Tonia cried a lot during the trip, mainly out of fear and exhaustion. Although I was extremely bitter towards her attitude, she needed to be consoled. It was difficult to cope with the sea, especially the weather conditions.

Once we approached the border between Nigeria and Cameroon, we were arrested by Nigerian sea patrol forces. We were taken to shore and told to get off the boat. Our boat was thoroughly searched for contraband, but they found nothing. The driver and captain were asked a few questions. Surprisingly, we were let go.

We spent a few more days at sea before we finally arrived on land. It was very early in the morning and we were told that a bus would pick us up in the afternoon to a place called: Oron Motor Park. We were told to hide in the bushes and remain quiet. The driver of the bus would find us where we were hiding. Once the instructions had been relayed, the boat that had taken us on our journey departed. Late in the afternoon, we heard a ruffling in the bushes.

'Do not be alarmed. All trips to Oron Motor Park.'

We got into the bus and made our way to the motor park. We had arrived in Oron.

Oron is a local government area in Akwa-Ibom state in Nigeria. It is a small town with a population close to 90,000 near to the Cameroonian border.

Before we arrived at the motor park, we were warned to hide our foreign currencies as this could attract suspicion from the roadside police at checkpoints. We had no choice. Tonia had to hide the little amount of money we had in her underwear. Once we arrived at the motor park, we took the night bus heading towards Ojuelegba bus stop in Lagos. When we arrived in Lagos, after a long drive, Tom and I separated. We would meet at the same bus stop in a month's time, as this was the same route I would be taking to return back to Gabon.

Tonia and I made our way to the boys' quarters' Vincent had left for me. The following day, I took Tonia to Tony's home.

'Thank God! I've been praying for her safe return,' Tony lamented very loudly.

Utterly surprised, I looked at Tony in disbelief. Why was he so happy and why was he praying for her return? I was expecting questions, not the jolly atmosphere I encountered. There was no regret on Tony's or Beki's face for her return. Had I been made to look like a fool? I didn't understand. I took Tonia to help my father and when I return with her in less than two months, I shouldn't be greeted with jubilation, but with unhappiness and concern. Yet, I was. Tonia had made me physically and mentally exhausted. But more than that, I was embarrassed. It was like Tony and Beki were expecting her return. I was saddened. I left them in their joy.

Once I left Tony's home, I went to look for Matthew. Before arriving home, we stopped to see Samantha. Everyone was surprised to see me, especially since I'd only been away for a few weeks. Nonetheless, it was good to spend time with her and her family. Weeks passed by rapidly and it had now been a month since my first arrival at Ojuelegba bus stop. I couldn't wait to return back to Gabon. I was running out of cash very fast and in a few more days, I would have next to nothing. I arrived early in the morning and waited and waited and waited. Still, Tom was nowhere to be found. I couldn't believe it. Where was he? Surely, he hadn't abandoned me in Nigeria. I couldn't phone him or visit him because I didn't have his number or address. I thought about making it back myself when I saw the bus to Oron, but I hardly knew my way there or who to speak to. I needed Tom and he wasn't there.

I came back day after day and still Tom didn't turn up. I decided to take a short trip to the North to visit Joy. Perhaps, when I came back, Tom would realise he had left his friend. I returned a few days later and found out that Tom had come looking for me. It hurt that I wasn't there. Days continued to pass and I had the smallest amount of cash possible. Gari and peanuts became my meals every morning and night for more than a week. Gari was a popular West African food made from cassava tubers, but it was also cheap enough to buy every day with the money I had, and to keep me alive. I would soak the Gari in pure water and then eat the salted and roasted peanuts with it. Eating it once or twice on occasion was nice, but eating it every day, twice a day for more than a week, I began to repel it. In addition to my eating problems,

I had no way of contacting Mama Cathy about my situation and tell her why I'd spent so long in Nigeria. There didn't seem like a way out. I tried to visit Samantha if she could help, but she had travelled to the UK. I was hopeless and helpless.

I had now spent almost three months in Lagos. No money, no food, no help. Could I have returned to Tony's home? No chance. What about Mary? I didn't want to alarm her. I tried to find a way to get in touch with Mama Cathy, but I knew I was just being stupid. My situation was dire. Was there a point in life if all you ever did was survive? When would I actually live life?

On that fateful day, I thought about taking my life. In my solitude, I began to reminisce about my past and to drop deeper and deeper into a state of depression. I began to question my life; I began to question whether God really existed. Drinking a whole bottle of Schnapps, I drowned my body in sorrow. I lay unconscious for two days.

'Peter, Peter.'

'I thought I was dead,' I said.

'Peter, Peter,' the voice continued. 'It's me, Tom!'

'Tom?' I wearily replied.

'Yeah. Let's get you off the bed and dressed.'

I was heavily dazed. I was vomiting incessantly, and I felt so light. I had no control over my body. I'd never drunk more than one glass of beer in my life, so I knew I would be like this for a few days.

Once I had freshened myself, Tom explained how he had fallen very ill and it was impossible for him to travel anywhere. He had come looking for me, but I was away. He asked what happened to me and I explained everything I had been going through, but I was so happy to see him. Finally, I would be going home. Tom stayed with me for three more days before we left to Oron. He didn't want to leave me alone at home. On the brink, I had survived again. But now, I was taking the same route back home. Life just wasn't fair.

Chapter 16: The Vanishing Trick

As soon as Tom and I arrived in Oron, we were told that the boat had just left for Gabon and they didn't know when the next boat would arrive. Tom and I looked at each other in disbelief. We couldn't quite believe that we had missed the boat. It was late afternoon, and we were both very tired after our strenuous trip from Lagos. Night fall came as the hours elapsed. We hadn't planned to stay overnight in Oron so getting accommodation was difficult, to say the least. We began walking around the town looking for anyone's help, until we met Asiko. Asiko was a young man; fairly tall, with a loud booming laugh. His dark skin starkly contrasted his yellow eyes and his hair seemed to blend in with his skin so that he seemed almost bald. He also had a funny sense of humour and a warm heart. Hearing about our disappointment, he took us in.

Knowing when the next boat would come was difficult. The people who drove the boats were extremely secretive, constantly changing their locations to avoid detection. Only a few people in the town knew about the human smuggling that was occurring on Oron's shores, and so Tom and I both knew that returning back to Gabon would now be more difficult.

We were both penniless and to return to Lagos wasn't an option. Asiko sustained us for a week and during the time we began to search for any person who knew anything about the boats. Oron was a nice place, the people were largely friendly, but most people seemed to be in a hurry – as those who dwelled there would say, 'time is money'. A lot of people called Oron the 'dead end' as it was close to the Cameroonian border; to cross the sea and get to

Cameroon without dying was near impossible — it was called the 'dead end' for a reason.

Frankly, living in Oron must've been quite boring. Ultimately, there was nothing to do and, apart from the jobs run by small households and the various trucks and lorries that drove through every few hours, it was lifeless. The trees made more noise than the people. As Tom and I ventured into the heart of the town, the strong stares of people made us feel like strangers. In the distance, we saw the Oron area boys. Tom and I quickly began to speak with them, and soon we became friends, or so we were given the impression – they don't take to kindly to strangers.

During our visit into the centre of town, we met a man willing to give us a place to stay. We thanked Asiko greatly for his kindness and left. The man took us into his home and pointed to the floor in the corner of his living room.

'That's where you'll be staying,' he told us. 'Make yourselves comfortable.'

Usually, I'd begin to feel sorry myself and continuously moan to Tom about how hard the floor was, but I was just happy to have a roof over my head. At least I wouldn't be outside in the unfriendly cold. Our only concern was how we were going to eat. The following morning, we decided to meet the area boys for help.

Surprisingly, it was easier than our first visit. They began to like us more and soon our rapport was comfortable. We told them about our situation and how we got into town. They seemed neither bemused nor shocked. In fact, it was a regular occurrence for young men like us to miss the boat. When we asked about how long these young men stayed in Oron before they found a boat, the reply was terrifying.

'It depends. It could be a few days, a few years and like my friend over here…his whole life.'

There was no way I was staying in Oron for longer than a month — and absolutely no way that I would be staying for my whole life. We needed to find a way to leave. Meanwhile, the area boys helped us get food and water and we ate until we were satisfied. Gradually, the area boys were no longer our distant friends, we were part of them.

Two months passed and I was still in Oron.

'What happened to only a month?' Tom slyly remarked one day.

There was no hope of returning. Tom and I had scouted practically the entire village for answers, information, even the smallest hint of when a boat would come. Yet, there was nothing. We'd heard of a boat from Oron being capsized on the Gabonese coast after being arrested by the Gabonese maritime police and tensions were rising in the town for fear of a police investigation. If that happened, there would definitely be no way to return to Gabon. Tom didn't share my cynical and pessimistic outlook and the news of a boat drowning at sea didn't bother him.

'It happens all the time,' he said.

But I still worried; how long were we to be fed by others? How long were we not to know when we would return? How long were we to live like men without hope? Tom was always the man with the plan, but this time there was no plan. It seemed like his continuous optimism was beginning to cloud his realism with his belief that we would somehow find our way back to Gabon. But as the days progressed, it began to dwindle until it became nothing.

Three months. By now, we were hearing that security on the sea had been tightened. There were an increasing number of stories coming back of how people were being killed at sea, perhaps aided by the maritime police when dying, perhaps not. But to Tom, they were all rumours. I only blamed myself for bringing Tonia to Gabon; I caused it, and now I was suffering the consequences. The shame of begging for food meant that we ate half a meal a day to survive. Sometimes, we visited the homes of our friends and ate there. After a while, our visits nearly three to four times a week were unwelcome. I wondered whether two bottles of Schnapps would do the trick to rid me of my pain completely; numb me mentally and physically. It would slow the transmissions across my synapses and reduce my reactions to nothing. I would be in a motionless state of nothing. As the toxins built up in my kidneys and my blood pressure began to rise, I would stare into the distance at nothing. And drawing my last breath, as I would pass away, I would say: 'Goodbye world, you won.'

'Good evening.'

Causing me to snap out of my daydream as I was lying on the floor, I was greeted with an unfamiliar voice.

'Good evening,' I replied.

I lifted my head to see the face of the person speaking to me.

'How are you?'

'I'm dying, but apart from that I couldn't be better,' I said standing up from the floor.

She giggled.

'Are you hungry?'

'Are you a mind reader?'

She smiled.

The whole situation seemed a little weird and overwhelming. With erratic eating patterns food was always on my mind. I was a ravenous, starving, malnourished, twenty four year old man, in desperate need of food and on the brink of suicide for a second time. Hungry was just not a good enough word.

'Why d'you ask?' I ask her, tempting a response.

'I know you're hungry and I also know you're waiting for a boat to Gabon.'

A sudden panic came over me, only a few people knew that Tom and I were in Oron to get a boat. That information was limited to perhaps only a few area boys and now this woman knew. 'What's your name?'

'John.'

Hesitant, she replied.

'How many of you are here?'

'Just me,' I replied, unsure of what would happen next.

She then began pacing left to right in the living room, picking things up and dropping them. She was smartly dressed. If I'd known any better, I'd probably say she was working for the state police. But there was something odd about her that led me to think otherwise; she smiled too much.

'Interesting. How long have you been here?'

'A few days at best.'

'When do you intend to leave?'

'Tomorrow.'

My responses were quicker than a bullet.

'You have money?'

'Shedloads.'

'Where is it?'

'Why should I tell you?'

She moved forward.

'Because if you don't, I might make your life a misery.'

'It already is,' I replied slowly.

'You know, a lot of you boys come over here to Oron to cross the border.' She continued after a brief pause. 'In fact, it's almost as regular as your compulsive lying. Isn't it Peter?'

'My name's not Peter.'

'Oh, isn't it?'

'No, it's John.'

'Well Peter, my name's Kate and welcome to Oron.'

Confused, I looked at her in silence. Her smile was concealing something more.

'Oh, don't be alarmed. I do this act all the time. It's just fun for me.'

'What is?'

'You know, tricking people that I know their next moves.'

'Is it a trick?'

'Are you still hungry or was that a lie too?'

'Yeah it was.'

'Oh you're a terrible liar. Did you ever do drama in school?'

'No.'

'At least you now have an excuse,' she continued. 'Follow me Peter.'

She was a beautiful young woman, full of smiles and wit. In fact, she was rather charming. For almost a second, I thought about following her. But I couldn't. I had to look for Tom. Running away from Kate, I found him in the kitchen with Asiko.

'There is a woman in the living room!' I shouted.

'Ah you've found Kate,' Asiko said. 'That was quick…First impressions?'

'Tom, could you explain to me what is going on?'

'Has she pulled out a knife, gun, or a sharp object with the intent to cause you harm?'

'What kind of a question is that?! There is a woman in the living room interrogating me!'

I heard Kate's footsteps get closer as she began to whistle.

'She knows that we've come to Oron to get a boat,' I whispered. 'And she wants me to follow her to go get something to eat.'

'What's wrong with you Peter?' Asiko asked. 'She's a young beautiful girl, with a warm heart. She's asked you to follow her and you're moaning like a little girl.'

'Am I the only one who sees this situation as a little weird?'

'Kate is the girl of the people. She's the darling of Oron and look at you. You're running away like a coward.' Asiko replied.

'What's with these comparisons Asiko?'

'Nothing. But when you can't tell a girl likes you, it's like meeting Arnold Schwarzenegger and not knowing who he is.'

'Now she likes me?!...And no, it isn't like that Asiko.'

'Just go with her and find out what she's up to.'

Tom intervened.

'Look Peter, if you don't want to go, fine. I'll take your place. Free food and an invitation, that's right up my street.'

'You're funny Tom.'

After some forceful persuasion, Tom and Asiko managed to convince me to follow her. Leaving the kitchen, I found her in the living room, sitting down on the chairs.

'I hope you still have an appetite,' she said.

'Let's go.'

Happily, she stood up and I followed her to her home.

Kate had a warm, cosy home. Her parents, Mr and Mrs Akpan, were very welcoming. It was easy to tell where Kate's smile had come from. I met more of Kate's family and their friends. It was almost like a party had been arranged with the amount of people in her home. During the meet and greets, I'd lost Kate to the kitchen. Meanwhile, one of the Akpan's family friends brought in some beer for everyone to drink. *Guinness*. I'd never tasted Guinness before in my life and at first it tasted like wood, if I ever knew how wood tasted…The warmth I was treated with was incredible. It was like I was part of their family, like they had known me for my whole life. Yet, I had only met them for a matter of minutes.

'Peter,' Kate shouted. 'The food's ready.'

The meal was a native dish to the people of Akwa Ibom state: Edikaikong soup with fufu or ẹbà, and was refuted to be one of the best dishes in North-Western Nigeria. It was used to either welcome guests or for a woman to trap her husband. I was told that the dish could resurrect a dying man. I asked Kate's parents what was in the soup and received a comprehensive reply.

'Ugu or as some people say pumpkin leaves; waterleaf; crayfish; smoked catfish fillets. What else? Ah. Giant snails; goat meat; kpomo; salt; pepper; palm oil; a few onions; some periwinkle and good old water. It's the best food in North-West Nigeria my boy!' Mr Akpan said enthusiastically.

'Best dish in North-West Nigeria?' I thought. 'We'll see about that.'

The beauty of the dish surrendered my propriety as I began to gluttonously tear apart the goat meat on my plate. It was the best meal of my life.

'You look like someone from my past,' Kate said.

'Well that would be hard. I don't even know who you are. Right now, you could be a Gabonese secret operative or a chef. But I'd like to think a chef as you've just cooked the most aromatic and flavoursome food I have ever tasted.'

She laughed, but it was almost mixed with disappointment. She knew I noticed.

'You're quite weird aren't you?'

'Likewise, Kate. Likewise.'

We became silent again as we ate the meal. She tried hard not to talk to me while I was eating; perhaps my beamy eyed glare at the food put her off. Once I nearly finished my meal, I asked her a question.

'Who do I like from your past?'

'A friend.'

'Sounds like more.'

'Just a friend.'

After the meal, everyone sat down together and began sharing jokes. It soon got dark, and I had to be on my way home; Tom would be concerned. Before I left, Kate gave me a potful of the edikaikong soup; she said it was for Asiko, Tom and I to share. I thanked her for the meal and the extra food she had given.

'You're weird Kate, but you're more kind.'

The more time I spent in Oron, the longer the thought of remaining in the town lingered. But I didn't stop searching for a boat that would take me back to Gabon. In the interim, Kate was doing her best to keep us entertained. She had an extremely funny sense of humour and enjoyed playing little pranks. She would make me laugh so much during a day that I would forget that Oron wasn't my home. Finding food to eat was no longer a problem for Tom and I; Kate was always there. She was very beautiful, so it came as no surprise to me that some of the area boys were vying for her attention. Sometimes, Kate and I would be walking on the streets together and we'd meet a few area boys. As they would try to flirt with her, she would convince them that I was her boyfriend.

It came to a point that almost the entire village believed I was her boyfriend. Even Tom began to question me and thought I was lying when I said there was nothing between us. At first, I thought it was a joke, just to make sure the area boys didn't approach her, but her seriousness started to make me think that Asiko was right about her.

With the number of visits to her home, I could essentially be called her boyfriend. And as it came more apparent to me that she did have feelings for me, my love for her was also beginning to grow. As each day passed, our friendship would reach another level. I had spent over five months in Oron and there was no sign of a boat. Was there a point in having hope? Kate was making me happy and I was having a glorious time.

One day, early in the morning, I was woken up by Tom. The elation and happiness on his face was unusual. He hadn't smiled for longer than five seconds in five months.

'What is it?' I asked. 'You sound like you've managed to get a boat or something.'

He stopped laughing and looked straight into my eyes.

'That's exactly what I've done.'

'Look Tom, it's very early and I know you and Kate were planning a trick on me, Asiko told me.'

'We dropped that idea weeks ago. Peter, we're going home. The boat is leaving tonight.'

'How d'you manage to get the boat?'

'A lot of hard work.'

'That's great; I'll meet you at Asiko's place.'

'Are you okay Peter?'

'Yeah, I'm fine…I'm just overwhelmed, that's all.'

'Then, you'll be happy to know that you're coming with me right now. We have to prepare.'

'Woah, relax Tom. We're leaving tonight. We still have time.'

'Are you drunk Peter? Because I think I'm being very serious.'

'It's 7am in the morning, how can I be drunk?'

'I'm surprised. I thought you would be jumping out of your bed and getting ready to go. We've spent five months in the middle of nowhere and you're acting like you want to stay now. What's wrong with you? Get dressed and let's go!'

The worst thing was that I didn't want to go. I'd begun to get used to life in Oron. At first, perhaps I didn't want to stay, but now I had Kate, I was enjoying myself, why would I want to leave?

'You know what Tom, you go. I'll catch up with you later. I need to get ready.'

'You better find me.'

'I will, I will.'

At that, Tom left.

Once I finished getting ready and was about to leave in search for Tom, I heard someone knock on the door.

'Oh, hi Kate.'

'Hi Peter. You okay?'

'Yeah, I'm fine.'

'What you up to today?'

'Nothing. But I'd really like a first class tour of the town.'

Smiling awkwardly she replied.

'Why do you want to do that? I've asked you so many times before and you've said no.'

'There's nothing to do today, so why not?'

I knew this was a perfect opportunity not to meet Tom. I knew we would come back late, and by then, Tom would have left for

Gabon without me. I knew if I told Kate that I was leaving she would try and persuade me to return. There was no way I was leaving — absolutely no way.

We returned very late at night as I had planned. We were told that Tom and Asiko had come looking for us several times. Kate was concerned and wondered why I'd not met up with Tom at Asiko's place if he'd asked.

'Are you hiding anything from me?'

'No.'

'You were always a terrible liar.'

Kate pushed me to talk, but I refused to.

'Please, you've got to do me a favour.'

'What?'

'If Tom and Asiko come looking for me, please tell them I'm not in.'

'You've got to be joking.'

As I was about to reply, someone knocked on the door. It was Kate's sister. They began speaking in the Oron dialect.

'Why didn't you tell me?'

'What?'

'Stop with the act. You know very well what. Why didn't you tell me?'

I moved towards her, held her hands, looked straight into her eyes and spoke slowly.

'You should know why.'

I knew she was right, but I'd lost interest in returning to Gabon. I could hardly remember that I even had Samantha. What more could be said when you were in love. Kate became furious.

'I can't believe this, Peter. What are you doing?'

The conversation grew into an argument. There was no way I was leaving. By now Tom should have left for Gabon. It was 11pm at night. Annoyed, Kate left me alone at home. I was nervous and distracted. I was concerned about where Kate had gone especially. I just hoped she wasn't going to visit Asiko. Quarter of an hour later, Kate came in again.

'I was worried. Where have you been?'

Kate was in an unhappy mood and I could understand why.

'Asiko's place is locked up. I think they've gone to the boat already.'

To me, it was brilliant news. My plan had worked. But for Kate, it was perhaps the stupidest thing I'd done since she'd met me. I could tell she was hurt by my actions.

'How could you?'

The real question was: how couldn't I? I knew I had some repair work to do, so I figured it was best to begin at that moment.

'I'm sorry that you feel this way.'

'Sorry?'

'You've looked after my friends and me for the past four months and you've always been there for me.'

'That doesn't mean you miss your boat.'

I knew how she felt, but she'd given me the affection and care that I missed. In Oron, I was happy with her. I smiled all the time, I ate the best meals of my life and I had a lot of friends. If I needed a job, I could get one from a local friend or Kate's family. I didn't think a life in Oron was that bad. As I began to explain to her my feelings, it seemed she understood my position a little better.

'But you've got to move on with your life. What about work and education? Oron is an isolated town. Nothing happens here. But you, you can travel, so why not?'

I explained to her that I didn't care anymore. I had her and Oron was a nice place to settle down.

'Who needs money when you have love?'

'So what are we going to do now?'

Finally, she accepted my position.

'Brilliant. Now you're talking.'

She laughed.

'We're staying together,' I said, apprehensive of her next reply.

'Okay,' she smiled.

My euphoria and ecstasy was huge, but I wasn't quite sure about her sudden change in reaction. Was I falling for one of her tricks again? But her smile thwarted my thinking.

The following day was like any other. It was marvellous to see Kate so happy. We ate my new favourite meal of edikaikong soup in the evening. Tom was nowhere to be found, and with no news of Asiko, it seemed like he must've joined Tom. By now, they would be deep into the sea. I was upset with myself for not saying a proper goodbye to Tom, but I had no other option, especially when he would never have let me stay. I was lost in Oron, but I loved it.

I decided to spend the night at Kate's home. Late in the evening, at about 8pm, one of Kate's uncles arrived, saying that Kate's sister was in trouble on the other side of the town. It was over two miles away and we had to hurry. Immediately after hearing the news, Kate rushed out.

'Peter, come with me. Hurry up. My sister's in trouble.'

Tension was high. Everyone was scared; no one knew what kind of trouble Kate's sister was in. I didn't hesitate to help after hearing Kate's invitation. It was tremendously dark and we couldn't see anything. We drove for about thirty minutes. Every so often, we would urge the driver to hurry. I offered to go by foot, but Kate said we would travel quicker by car. At one point, we went off the road and drove through the forest. We drove for a while longer, until the driver told us that his vehicle could go no further. Surprisingly, the driver and Kate's uncle failed to get out of the car.

'We'll wait here and make sure everything is okay. She's just over there,' said Kate's uncle pointing to the bushes. 'It's only a few minutes away.'

Kate and I continued alone. Suddenly, out of nowhere, someone jumped out of the bushes. I didn't know what was going on. Ready to defend myself, I raised my arms ready to swing a punch. Immediately, Kate held my hands. I think he's here to help us.

'Come with me, they're here.'

Holding my hands, Kate and I ran behind the man very quickly. We were running very fast, and soon we arrived at a dead end. I thought we'd lost our way.

'Kate, is your sister okay?'

I began to get worried. Kate wouldn't tell me anything about her sister, where she was or what had happened to her. While discussing the issue, three men appeared with a very small boat.

'What's the boat doing here?'

'I'm sorry Peter, but you have to go.'

'You set me up?' I asked in disbelief.

'I'm sorry Peter.'

'I thought you loved me. I thought you were happy that I was staying with you.'

Tears of sadness began to flow down Kate's cheeks.

'I don't want to be the person who stops you from achieving your dreams, Peter. Your home isn't here. Go back. I'm sorry.'

'You're not stopping me. I want to stay here with you. It's my choice, not yours.

'We've got to go.'

It was Asiko.

'Asiko? I thought you'd gone.'

'Time's not on our side, you better jump into the boat now.'

'I thought you left yesterday night. Where's Tom?'

'You caused it. We should've left, but Tom insisted that you've got to come with us and refused to leave if we didn't promise to send you back.'

'So where is he?'

'He went with the boat you were meant to go in.'

I knew I had no other choice. If I tried to run away, perhaps they would catch me and bundle me into the boat with force. My hope to stay lost in Oron was over. I was going back. I turned to Kate.

'I guess you got what you wanted in the end.'

'You know how it is…I was always good at tricks.'

'How could you?'

'I'm sorry Peter. I know you like me. I like you too. But you've got to move on with your life…'

It was a tough moment. Perhaps she was right, perhaps there was something better for me in life, but I wanted to stay in Oron. I looked at it as my new home. The weight of sadness lowered my head as I walked into the boat. As Asiko began to paddle away from the shore, she shouted.

'Remember me, Peter!'

Twenty two hours later, Asiko and the two other men in the boat paddled over to a stream bank that cut into the sea. Surprised at where Asiko was going, I shouted.

'Where are you going?'

'Shhh, you'll blow our cover.'

Giving him the benefit of the doubt, I lowered my voice. Then in the midst of the overgrowing vegetation, I saw what appeared to look like a boat. As we got closer, I saw Tom. So this was where the main boat was. Asiko and I got into the boat, while the other two men left.

I didn't say a word to anyone, including Tom. I was upset with the world and myself. A few people in the boat called me 'loverboy', but for what it was worth, I did love her.

A few hours later, our boat moved out from the river and crossed back into the sea. Nothing could hide how upset I was. It was beginning to get cold at sea and Kate had packed a jumper for me to wear. As I was about to wear it, three pictures fell to the bottom of the boat. They were all pictures of Kate. They had planned it perfectly. To escape from my agony, I slept.

I woke up energised and tried to forget what had happened to me. We were moving very fast at sea, so it was only a matter of time before we would make it back to Gabon. Taking my mind away from Kate, I began to observe the wonders of the sea, how the fish jumped into the air, and the sun glistened on their skin as they would shake their tails. It was beautiful. The waves were terrifyingly powerful and swayed the boat from side to side. The journey was no different from my first; it would still rank amongst my worst experiences.

Within a matter of days, we arrived at Jege in the evening. We waited until it was late before we got off the boat. I had no real problem travelling in Gabon as I had my resident permit and passport with me. The seawater had damaged parts of my passport, but my permit was still intact. We stayed in Jege overnight and in the early hours of the following morning, Tom and I took a small boat to cross the 20 minutes to Coco beach.

If I hadn't realised earlier, I was now back in Gabon. It had been almost a year since I'd left, but the place hadn't changed. It still had the same smell, the same look and the same people. It felt good to be back. Tom and I went our separate ways from Coco beach. After taking a bus from a nearby motor park, I made my way home. Tom and I had left Asiko back in Jege. For those who didn't have a resident permit, it would be difficult to travel from Jege to Coco beach. There were over forty people in the boat and most would enter the country as illegal migrants. My heart ached for the people who carried out these journeys. As I made my way home through the streets of Libreville, questions were going through my head: would I ever see Kate again? What will Mama Cathy say when she sees me? Will she still go on about Jessica? When would I get back to Nigeria? There were too many things to think about, but for now, I just enjoyed being back home.

Chapter 17: Shaken, but Unhurt

Mama Cathy was relieved to see me back home, but the excitement and happiness of my return dissipated within twenty four hours.

'When are you going to marry Jessica?'

The same question over and over and over. I think Mama Cathy was forcefully trying to thrust the marriage of Jessica into my head so that it became my desire. The pressure she hurled at me hurt. I couldn't concentrate on education or my work, even if I tried my hardest to ignore her.

I soon became sick. The events of Oron and my first few days in Gabon had taken its toll on me. When I recovered, it was impossible to focus on anything. All Mama Cathy wanted me to focus on was Jessica. I began thinking to tell Mama Cathy that I already had Samantha. But to spring a surprise on her like that, would not only kill me, it would kill her too. She would never believe that I had married a woman in Nigeria. I then began to think about running away to an area where I would never be seen again, where I would be able to just live in peace without having to think about the commitments I'd made, where I could get another start. But I was just kidding myself. Reflecting on my life so far, I realised that I had made a lot of mistakes, but also I had learnt a lot. I'd been through every emotion possible and still managed to come out on the other side. The next step was facing my problems head on. I had to tell Mama Cathy about Samantha sooner or later.

It was mid-1995 and I think it would be fair to begin to describe myself as a fully grown adult. Life was hard, but it always is. You are always faced with a new problem every day, and sometimes it feels like the same problem won't go away. But even if there is no logical way out and it seems hope is lost, I've learnt that you need to make your own way. Because although it may seem like you've lost everything, as the adage goes: when there is will, there is *always* a way.

A few weeks after my return from Oron, while at work, I received a letter from Samantha. It'd been a while since I'd heard from her. Her letter was dated April 1995, but it was now mid-1995. Nonetheless, I read its contents with eagerness.

Dear Honey,

At home 10.05am, 27th April 1995

I love you darling. How was your trip to Gabon? Please make sure you get enough rest before you do anything. I thank God for his mercy on you. It's been so long since we've seen each other. I would love to see you again. And I don't mind coming with you to Gabon or Paris.

About the letters I've been sending you, I hope Callis has been delivering them to you. I love you. And please when we see again, I would like another ring from you.

Peter, can you believe that I'm having dreams about you? I want you desperately and we need to do an introduction soon. A picture of you is always by my bedside when I'm sleeping. I also keep my phone at my bed side as I await your call.

Please come and see me, I miss you loads. I love you.

Samantha.

Samantha now lived with her sister in the United Kingdom and this was the first time I'd received a letter from her since my return. It seemed like her love for me had not wavered even though I had been away for quite a while. In her letter, she said she needed another ring, but I wasn't quite sure why. She also said she wanted an introduction between her family and mine, whereby both families would be able to come together and speak more to each other. It was still a secret between Samantha and me about our marriage. And her message only exacerbated my thoughts about telling Mama Cathy. Mama Cathy was my family also. But I was so afraid of telling her because I knew if I did, perhaps I would lose her trust.

'You must only marry in the faith,' said Fefe.

Fefe would come to Mama Cathy's place and teach me about the creed and about how to get closer to God. He would teach me the rules of the rite as taken from the Bible. Fefe also spoke and taught English, but his first language was French. It made our Bible studies much easier, but it also meant that I was able to learn more French. We were doing my last lesson about the rules of the faith, when I began asking questions about marriage.

'But why not elsewhere?' I replied.

Marriage within our faith was a very important matter and you were not allowed or encouraged to marry outside of the faith. If you were one of the Jehovah's Witnesses, it was absolutely necessary that you got married to one of the witnesses. Sex before marriage was disallowed and marriage outside the faith was frowned upon. Mama Cathy was obstinate about me marrying in the faith, and that perhaps justified her inexorable propositions for me to marry Jessica. But whenever I thought about that rule, I thought of Jean, M'bembi's father, who had denied me the one woman I loved the most. M'bembi and I were both in the same faith, yet it was because I was a Nigerian that I was not permitted to marry his daughter.

As well as my Bible tutor, Fefe was a close friend to me and I discussed nearly everything with him. He knew about the issues with Jessica and M'bembi, but I really wanted to speak to him about Samantha. I thought about telling him that I married Samantha, but I knew what he'd say and he'd probably tell Mama Cathy about it also. And when that happened, I knew many mountains would fall at Mama Cathy's voice. The only thing I could never really understand was why some parents never allowed their children to marry those whom they loved, and never care what the consequences of their actions will be.

I needed to talk to someone about Samantha. I thought about Jibé, but he wouldn't take too kindly to the idea either, especially since we also both practiced the same faith. I knew very well that I would receive no support from anyone if they knew that Samantha wasn't one of the Jehovah's Witnesses. I knew I'd made a mistake, and it didn't feel good. Samantha kept sending letters and I knew I was under pressure to tell someone immediately. Samantha wanted to come to Gabon, but no one knew we were married.

Gradually, as days went by, it became easier to keep my relationship with Samantha a secret. But I knew it was only a matter of time before someone found out. I'd been hearing rumours that Samantha's sister, who Samantha was staying with in England, had found out that we had gotten married. One day, I received a phone call from Samantha.

'Hello Peter, it's me Samantha. Please call me back.'

Her anxious voice alerted my ears and I quickly returned the call.

'Hello, it's me.'

'I'm in trouble, they've found out.'

'Found out what?'

'Found that we're married.'

'How?'

'They found out from the phone bills and overheard one of our conversations.'

She paused.

'The bills were over £200.'

'£200! You're joking.'

I couldn't believe the amount Samantha had spent. Perhaps it was rather extreme, but I guess that's the lengths you go to when you want to speak with the one you love. It was terrible that the sum was so large, and I wanted to know what happened next.

'My sister has told my parents and we're in a lot of trouble.'

I knew that I had caused a lot of problems when I failed to tell anyone about our marriage. But it wasn't fair. Why couldn't we marry who we wanted to? Whether it was religion, prejudice, culture, society or anything else for that matter, there was always an obstacle stopping you from getting what you wanted, what you desired. Perhaps what I did wasn't the right thing to do, perhaps it was a mistake, but it didn't matter anymore. I had married Samantha and now there was nothing anyone could do about it.

Samantha received the brunt of the insult, particularly from her parents. Everyone in her family disapproved of our marriage, apart from Nuru, and her elder sister, Kike. Samantha's parents disapproved of us, but Kike believed that our marriage wouldn't have been secretive if we'd been allowed to marry when we wanted to. All I could do was console Samantha. I begged for forgiveness if I'd caused her any unwanted embarrassment.

'My dad and mum have written me. My sister has also found the ring you sent me. They disagree with our marriage and I'm not sure if we should continue or not.'

The panic and sadness in her voice weighed heavily on my mind. She was hugely troubled, but I was nowhere near her to give her the comfort she needed. Suddenly, the emotion in her voice rose and the tears rolled down her cheeks even more.

'What is it? Have they hurt you? Are you okay?'

'I'm fine,' she sobbed heavily.

'C'mon you can tell me.'

'I didn't mean to do it.'

'Do what?'

I couldn't understand what she was trying to tell me.

'I didn't know what I was doing. I sat on the floor. I didn't know. I tore it apart…'

'Tore what apart? I don't understand. What's happened Samantha? Say it slowly.'

'They wouldn't stop insulting me. I ran to the balcony…'

'Have they hurt you? What's happened?'

'I'm sorry Peter, I'm sorry.'

'Samantha, I really need you to tell me what's happened. I don't know what you're talking about.'

She stopped crying for a moment. Sniffling, she spoke.

'I tore it apart Peter.'

'What did you tear apart?'

There was a long silence.

'Our marriage certificate.'

It was as if I was in paralysis. I couldn't move. She started speaking on the phone again, but even though my ears were on the phone, I wasn't listening. I was thinking. I thought about whether

I'd rushed into marriage, whether she was dragged into a decision she was not prepared for. She had torn apart our marriage certificate in her own hands. I couldn't understand. Later on, when I had managed to wake my brain, she told me that her family pushed her over the edge. They were repeatedly having a go at her and out of desperation for sanity, she ripped it apart. But in my head nothing could excuse tearing apart our marriage certificate.

From that day forward, I thought our relationship would be seriously affected. Samantha was hugely apologetic, but for me it was perhaps the worst thing that had happened in my life till then. I couldn't tell whether it was the end of our relationship and the impact it would have in the future. I didn't know what to do anymore. There were just so many things happening.

Time passed and I tried to make myself forget about what had happened that day. Samantha insisted on an introduction between both families, but I couldn't see what difference it would make. Moreover, I had to think about how to resolve the Jessica problem, and forsake my attraction to M'bembi. I didn't know what I was doing. Perhaps, I'd also done some things wrong, but I had no one to tell me. Everything had been a secret and now I was suffering the consequences.

It had been almost two years since I'd heard from Mary and I really needed to speak with her. It seemed like the introduction would actually be happening very soon, so I needed Mary's advice. I'd made a lot of mistakes and I knew Mary would help me focus my thoughts better. Somehow, Samantha's parents were much more accepting of our marriage, perhaps because it was already done, but I was glad we were making progress. They wanted to see my parents and I knew I had to tell Tony and the family about this.

Whenever Samantha and I discussed the issue of the introduction, I couldn't help to think that I was never really wanted. But what troubled my heart the most was the fact that Samantha had torn our marriage certificate apart, even if it was an act influenced by her family. For me, it was like telling me they disliked me; they were rejecting me. She could have yielded to their persuasion or coaxing, she could have firmly held her ground, but she didn't.

February 1996. Samantha had arrived in Nigeria from England, and was also expecting me to arrive soon from Gabon. While I was preparing, Vincent was working out a plan to make it a memorable occasion. Expectantly, I was nervous about the entire arrangement. Was I completely sure about what I was about to do? I still hadn't told anyone in Gabon about Samantha, and now things were getting even more serious, if it wasn't before.

One day, while at my place of worship, my eyes crossed paths with M'bembi and the look in her eyes told me everything. There was something about the look that told me she still loved me. Even though I may never have been certain, something told me she still loved me. And truthfully, I still loved her. In my head, I began blaming myself for my irrationality, but now there was no way out. I had completely messed myself up, and now I would be heading to Nigeria to join Samantha for our introduction.

Samantha's parents only lived a few hundred metres away from where I stayed and I knew Vincent and I would have to hurry to get things sorted out. It was good to see Samantha again. I thought it would be awkward, especially after what had happened, but I forced myself to forget. When I settled my bags, I quickly went to see Mary in the village to explain my whole situation. I also hoped to see some of Elizabeth's brothers and sisters, as I was yet to be introduced to them. I had also heard that my biological mother had other children: Maria, her first daughter, and Jude, her first son. I was told that she had had those children before she had gotten married to Tony. I hoped to see them, but Mary was my biggest priority. She stood by me like any mother would do to a son; she was an exceptional woman.

As I travelled to Akarakunmo, the village Mary lived and I had grown up in from an early age, I began to hear of rumours about Mary. People had been calling her a witch, and even Vincent believed it. I was warned by people not to visit where she lived. All of a sudden, all the most vile and cruel things were associated with my mother. It was terrible to hear people curse her, and tell deplorable stories. Some said she was the cause of all the misfortune and illness in the village. Some said she was the cause of all deaths in the village. Some of the stories were so fictitious I felt like hurling a punch into someone's face. I couldn't believe the extents that people I didn't even know were going to, to convince me not to visit Mary.

I couldn't understand why people were being so impolite, disrespectful and insolent towards my mother. She wouldn't have a hurt a single soul, yet they were calling her an evil woman and a witch. I couldn't believe that Tony hadn't even said anything on the matter, or even tried to defend his sister. Instead, he said nothing, perhaps also in quiet agreement with the rumours circulating the village.

I vowed Mary would come to the introduction, especially after the hurtful things that had been said about her. Mary was the opposite of every contemptible adjective they hurled upon her. When I told certain people that Mary was coming to my introduction, they roared in disapproval, telling me I was insane and warned me not to invite her. My temper was beginning to rise and what they were saying was now completely unacceptable. How could they warn me not to bring my mother to my introduction? They told me how they feared that the woman who had protected me through my childhood was going to harm me. The worst thing was they blamed the death of Vincent's son on her. No wonder Vincent thought she was a witch! Mary was a childless, helpless woman, who was carelessly abandoned in the village. She received rare visits only from Janet, Tai and Vincent. But I don't even think Vincent would have stepped foot in Mary's home for a while. I didn't know what to do. That seemed to me to be a familiar tale in my life — not knowing what to do.

There was constant humiliation everywhere I went. Every time I said the name Mary, people looked at me, looked around and then said 'Don't say the name of that witch.' I needed to find out what was going on. I knew what I was about to do was probably the worst thing I could do to the mother I loved, but I guess it was also for my sanity, more than anything.

I was with Matthew and Vero, my half-sister, when I went to see Mary. I ignored the various attempts to prevent me from seeing her and went to her home. Once she caught sight of me, Mary began to cry and lament.

'No one has come to see me my son. I have been abandoned, left alone to die in this world. Everyone is frightened of me, saying that I'm an evil witch. Peter, am I an evil witch?'

She nearly fell to floor, as I used my arms to keep her upright. She was even weaker than the last time I'd seen her. It never did me any good when I saw Mary cry out of pain; especially after all she'd gone through for my sake.

'Are you practicing witchcraft?'

She looked into my eyes, searching for hope, in disbelief at what I had asked.

'Do you really believe that I'm a witch?'

'The news is everywhere. Do you know how many people warned me not to visit you? Do you know how many people said that I was the son of a witch? Do you know what people say about you? What can I believe mother?'

What I had said was unbearable for her. The tears that flowed onto her frail cheeks made me want to cry also, but I had to be sure. In my heart, I cried at the thought that I had allowed myself to doubt my mother. She was the only woman who truly cared about me since my birth, and look at what I was saying. I looked at her again. She was crying and with every breath she took, it felt like she was slipping away. As I was about to speak again, Janet's father, Afini walked in.

'It's hatred,' he said.

Afini had grown hugely annoyed at the way Mary had been labelled by the village as a witch. Janet and Tai were now living with Mary and they were all happy together, but I couldn't understand what caused an entire village to believe that my mother was a witch. I was even told that Mary's next door neighbour believed she was a witch. Out of anger, I ran outside of the house and stood in the middle of the path that led towards Mary's front door. I wanted to be heard by the entire village and I wanted my message to spread. I wasn't afraid to defend my mother at risk of death or injury, because Mary was prepared to do the same for me. In a loud voice, I shouted.

'YOU MUST ALL STOP THIS NONSENSE NOW! MY MOTHER IS NOT A WITCH AND WILL NEVER BE A WITCH. IF ANYONE PERSISTS CALLING HER SUCH NAMES, I WILL

COME FOR YOU…I WILL FIND YOU…AND THEN GOD HELP YOU.'

I went inside and had a serious conversation with Tai, Janet and Mary.

'I should have eaten you all when you were younger if I was a witch,' Mary said.

Mary wouldn't have hurt the tiniest creature created. Instantly, I made sure to tell Mary why I'd asked her whether she was a witch.

'Mama, I never believed you were a witch. That is why I came to see things for myself. I couldn't have believed people who knew nothing about you so easily. I just needed to ask for my sanity.'

I later informed Mary about Samantha, but didn't tell her anything that had happened. She was so weak and I didn't want to hurl my problems upon her, when she was involved in one already. Mary was happy that I had gone for Samantha, especially after what she had told me when we both came to visit, but I also had to tell her what people had said regarding her appearance at my introduction.

'Mama, people told me that I should not allow you to come to my introduction, because you would gobble everyone up, including me.'

She laughed.

'Of course, that's what they'll say.'

But I couldn't help to think that all the people who had discouraged me to invite Mary, who else would they have suggested to replace her? Mary was my mother and if they didn't like her at my introduction, quite frankly, they were not invited. To me, she would always be my mother. It was customary for a father and mother to be present at the introduction ceremony of their child. If Mary wasn't there, who was meant to be this mother? They must've been dreaming if they thought I would deny Mary from attending my introduction. Mary meant a lot to me and she would be at my introduction — no matter the cost.

It was getting late and I soon met up with my cousin Bino. Bino lived with his parents opposite Mary's house. Bino and I planned a way to ensure that Mary was at my introduction. It was great to see everyone again, including Mary. Although what I encountered on my return was terrible to deal with, I'd seen my mother again. That night, I made my way back to the city.

The following morning, Vincent confronted me about my visit to Mary. The news had spread across the village that I'd visited 'the home of the witch'. He was furious with what I'd done and thought that I would die before the next evening because of the announcement I'd made in the village. I felt a bit proud of what I'd done. As hoped, my message had spread across the village. I smirked at the thought of people deliberating over what I'd done.

'Why are you smiling? You could have got yourself killed. Why did you visit her?'

'Why do people make a big fuss from nothing? I went to see my mother. I don't think there's a big problem with that.'

Our conversation soon ballooned into an argument. As Vincent tried to persuade me that Mary was a witch, I interrupted him.

'This has got to stop now. Mary is not a witch. And I'd prefer you stopped saying that *bro*.'

I was unhappy with Vincent's attitude. The worst thing was that he had resolved not to attend my introduction if Mary was present. I couldn't understand why there was so much venom towards her. It seemed to be so unfounded.

The next day, Samantha and I quickly began planning the introduction. A date was fixed and our attire had been selected. We were both going to wear a traditional Nigerian outfit for the introduction, although, we were yet to purchase the textiles. As we were travelling on the roads, there was a huge amount of traffic on Orile/Mile 2 road. Policemen were stopping and searching cars and their work was painstakingly slow, leaving us wondering what was going on. As we made our way towards Orile Bridge, our car was pulled to the side of the road by the police officers.

'Good afternoon. What do you have in your boot?'

'Nothing officer,' our driver replied.

Another officer began to shout.

'Get out of your car! Get out of your car!

We all exited the car and stood at the side of the road. The police officers led the driver to the boot of the car and asked him to open it. The car was checked thoroughly as if we were criminals, but they found nothing. One of the police officers then confronted me.

'Hey you, open your wallet.'

I didn't speak, but I refused to open my wallet. At seeing my defiance, he started to fire his gun into the air. Another officer in military uniform also began to fire into the air. Both men then began to shoot at the floor near my feet. We didn't know what was going on. Why would the police ask me to open my wallet? We then began to suspect that they weren't police, but armed robbers.

'Stop!' Lanre shouted.

Lanre was one of my cousins, who had accompanied us on our trip. Once he said this, he was slapped repeatedly by the officers and then bundled into their ostensible police van. After being threatened at gun point, I opened my wallet. As I did so, I was thrown into their police van. But I was not beaten. Samantha began crying and urged the fake police officers to let Lanre and I go. People were looking at us, but nobody helped. To everyone else, the police were doing their job; they were simply arresting suspected criminals.

Some of the police men went into our car, while they seated Samantha in the back. They separated Lanre and I from Samantha and drove off. I was terrified. I thought we were going to die. They were going to take all our money and kill us. They were mindless; we were ordered not to talk. And if we did…

'One gunshot to the head,' one of the police officers warned.

We were taken to their hideout, only a few hundred yards away from the bridge, and only a few metres away from the National Theatre, opposite Orile Bridge. When we got there, we were ordered out of the van, while they checked my briefcase thoroughly. After searching through my passport, they knew I didn't reside in Nigeria. And although I hid my money carefully in case of any eventuality, they found 10,000 CFA Francs with me. They were very aggressive and furious that they had only seen that amount of money. Meanwhile, Samantha had joined up with us. She was crying and begging for mercy from the officers.

'Please let us go. We're here for our introduction. Please, let us go.'

Hearing that, one of the officers came up to me.

'Where are you from?'

After I'd given him my reply, the man who I believed to be the leader of the armed robbery group, had a short meeting with his colleagues and then ordered Lanre and I enter to enter his car. As I began approaching his car, one of the officers spoke.

'If you take one more step, I will shoot you.'

The leader of the group shouted at me.

'Enter the car now! Don't waste my time.'

I didn't know what to do. I was in a state of panic. Should I move forward or stop? I could feel the tension in everyone. An argument then ensued between the leader and the officer who had spoken. All of sudden, I don't know how, I summoned the courage to move forward and slowly moved into the car. Once the argument had died down, the leader came over to us.

'I'm sorry about that. These people are a bit crazy. They kill people at the click of a finger. But please give anything you can afford.'

I thought they were all crazy and felt like running them over with the car we were in, but I wasn't the driver and I didn't know how to drive. With no other choice, I gave them the 10,000 CFA Francs they had found.

'That is all I have.'

'We didn't force you to give us this money. You gave it to us out of your good will. We don't want you coming back here to make any trouble with us.'

What was this man saying? We were practically coerced into this decision. It was either that or death. When I handed the man the sum, we were escorted back onto Orile Bridge, given our car and then we drove off. We were mostly shaken, but unhurt. It was a dreadful experience. When we managed to get to Idumata and Tinubu market, we explained to people what had happened to us. Apparently, our incident wasn't rare. Many people had lost their lives that year from the barbarism of armed robbers that dressed as police officers. In haste, we bought the textiles we needed and quickly made our way home.

We thought about reporting the incident to superior authorities in the Nigerian police force, but by doing so, we'd scare Samantha's parents. Perhaps, the introduction would have been called off. Moreover, I only had a few more days to spend in Nigeria and I couldn't afford not having done the introduction. As a result, Samantha and I decided to keep it a secret. On our way back, we saw the same armed robbers on the bridge, but this time we hastily escaped their checkpoint and drove off at speed. However, we couldn't allow the incident to go unreported, so we decided to report what had happened at a local police station.

The day of our introduction ceremony was soon approaching, yet there were still things that had to be attended to. Meanwhile, one of Elizabeth's sisters, Rita, had been invited to the ceremony. I knew nothing of my biological mother, so perhaps it was fair to have someone related to her present at my introduction and to tell me more about her. I hardly knew where she came from. All I was told was that she came from Ogun State in Nigeria. I didn't even know Elizabeth's full name until Rita told me.

The day had finally arrived and it was great to see so many people at the occasion. Tony, Beki, Mary, two of Elizabeth's brothers, Emeka and Rita were present. I was happy to see them all together, but especially happy to see that Mary was present. The day was largely successful, and our happiness was easily noticed. The ceremony didn't finish until late. Because of the tension in the village, Mary couldn't travel home at night and so we decided for her to stay at Tony's place until the morning. I gave her a huge hug and waved her goodbye. She asked that I see her before I return to Gabon, and so I happily obliged.

Two days after our introduction, I began to get really ill. Samantha's mum kept me bed-ridden for treatment, while needles penetrated my rear. I was so ill that I nearly forgot my departure date. After checking my flight details, I realised that my flight was the following morning. Without a choice, I had to get ready to leave. I didn't want a repeat of the Oron journey, and this time there was no Tom to help me. Sadly, it meant that I couldn't go and see Mary as I'd promised; I just hoped that she'd understand. Two days after I left Nigeria, Samantha departed to England and insisted that she would soon join me in Gabon.

Although I had a splendid time at my introduction, I was still worried about Mama Cathy. My marriage with Samantha was now completely sealed. Samantha wasn't in the same faith as me and I knew Mama Cathy wanted me to marry in the faith. I knew there would be trouble, and I knew the longer I waited, the harsher her response would be. What was going to happen next? I began to search for an answer…

Chapter 18: Foolish Mr Fox

I knew I had to tell Mama Cathy about my relationship with Samantha. I'd kept it as a secret for so long from her and it was only fair that I told her. But the only thing was I knew what her response would be, and as much as I was willing myself to tell her, I couldn't. Mama Cathy had done so much for me, and even if I did find her ruthlessly exasperating regarding Jessica, I knew she was only doing so because she loved me. I was also facing increasing pressure from Samantha to arrive in Gabon. But if Samantha arrived in Gabon where was she going to reside? She couldn't reside with me at home, when I hadn't told Mama Cathy. I tried to stall her arrival as much as I could, but Samantha's threats were slowly snowballing into action. But candidly, in a situation like this, I couldn't be caught off-guard. I had to make sure Samantha arrived when I was ready. As sad as that may sound, I'd kept my marriage a secret from even my closest friends. So there was no way Samantha was coming without me agreeing.

As months continued, however, Samantha's persuasiveness started to sway me. It did seem a bit suspicious that I wasn't allowing her to come to Gabon. After all, we were married. So the more I said no, the less convincing my reasons became. It was only a matter of time before I would receive a phone call from Samantha telling me she was at Libreville's Leon M'ba Airport, and she was taking a taxi to my address. I needed to do something quickly, but what? That was the question. Should I tell Mama Cathy then suffer the consequences? No, because I'd ultimately get evicted and she'd lose her trust in me. Should I tell my best friends, Jibè and Fefe?

No, they'd probably have a go at me, tell Mama Cathy and ultimately I'd get evicted and she'd lose trust in me. Should I try and convince Samantha that she shouldn't come yet? Well, I'd being doing it for months and her patience was thinning — another excuse would be game over. I knew if my little — okay, large — secret got out, I'd lose face with Mama Cathy, my friends and even people at my place of worship. Moreover, what would M'bembi think? If she still loved me, would I have truly ended anything that we may have had? There were too many questions and too little time. My only option was to try and stall Samantha.

The phone rang. It was Samantha.

'Hi honey, how are you?'

'I'm fine darling, what about you?'

'I'm good, how's work going and things?'

'Oh, it's going good. Business is a bit slow right now, so I'm tight with money. There's nothing really much here.'

'Oh…That's a shame. I'm sure it will get better.'

'I pray it does.'

There was a pause.

'Have you thought about my arrival to Gabon recently?'

'You know what I said before. I'm just not financially ready yet. I hope you understand.'

'Oh of course, of course. That's why I've bought my own ticket to Libreville. I shall be with you soon my dear.'

'Oh, you've bought a ticket?'

'Yeah, I saved up a little and got one. You sound surprised?'

'Me? No…not at all. When are you coming?'

'Soon.'

'A date?'

'Oh, I need to re-check, I don't want to make a mistake.'

I had to do something; I certainly couldn't afford a surprise visit.

'You can't come.'

'What? Why?'

'Well, remember what I've told you before. You need to be in the same faith as me. You can't join me if we're not practicing the same religion.'

'You've got to be kidding me. I can't join you in Gabon because I'm not a Jehovah's Witness. Rubbish! What's that all about? For heaven's sake, we're married. Whenever you give me an excuse why I can't come, you sound like you're hiding something from me! Or *are you*?'

That was a question I couldn't answer. I knew I was hiding something from her, but imagine me telling her — that was never going to happen. After I successfully managed to dodge the question, we left the conversation on the note that she would be coming to Gabon; the only thing was I didn't know when. I was in a huge pile of mess and now I had to act. I was forced to act.

Matthew was now living with me in Gabon and I talked to him freely about my situation. It was easy to tell Matthew, he was family, and he was also one of my closest friends. Unlike Jibè and the others who'd probably reprimand me, Matthew just listened and gave me advice. Finally, I had someone to talk to about my problems. Matthew and I both worked at my block factory, so during my shifts, we'd converse. We then worked out a plan: I would lodge Samantha in a hotel or room for the moment, completely away from Mama Cathy's sight or anyone else's for that matter. I would be able to see her whenever I wanted and no one would find out a thing. Without delay, I rented a two bedroom flat about a mile away from where Mama Cathy and I stayed.

A week later, early September 1996, Samantha arrived in Libreville. It was great to see her again, especially since we'd last met in February. But after all my efforts to prevent her from coming, she was now in Gabon. Would this be the beginning of trouble? If I managed the situation effectively, I would be able to get away with it. Curious for how long I'd have to put on an act; I asked her when her return date was.

'I got a one-way ticket. I want to stay with you for as long as I can.'

Now that was not what I wanted to hear. A one-way ticket! I'd be foiled. I tried to keep calm and carry on with the plan, but I knew it would be difficult — very, very difficult.

After a short drive, I took her to the flat I'd rented. I stayed with her for several hours, before I left her alone in the apartment. In the nights, I had to return. That meant I wasn't sleeping my nights at Mama Cathy's place. I didn't know how long I'd be able to keep it up, but for the moment it was the only solution I had.

Managing my time between Samantha, work and Mama Cathy was demanding at the least. Samantha wanted to know why I hadn't taken her to Mama Cathy's place, since I'd told her before that Mama Cathy had taken me in, and I gave the excuse it was because she was a devoted Jehovah's Witness, which to an extent was true. Accepting my religion was almost the biggest nightmare for her and so I knew I could get away with that excuse. One evening, we were having a conversation, when Samantha said something that touched me.

'So this is it. I never bargained for this. Please tell me I won't be staying all alone in this flat? I want to meet your friends. This is like a prison. Peter, get me out!' she joked.

I laughed, but it was a laugh that pleased her more than it pleased me. I thought about telling her the truth about my situation, but she couldn't understand. So it was better not to. I'd managed to handle the situation and so there was no need to cause alarm.

So I thought I was in control of the problem, but really I wasn't. I no longer spent time at work because I had to be with Samantha, and it was difficult trying to think of an excuse for Mama Cathy as to why I wasn't sleeping at home. I knew, as the days advanced, it would only be a matter of time before someone found out.

After managing to escape from work one day, I went to see how Samantha was getting on. As usual, she complained about being stuck on her own. As I tried to mess about with her and make her smile, she spoke.

'I think I'm pregnant.'

My eyes blew up and my ears stood up.

'Could you repeat that again slowly?'

I heard her alright, but I wanted to be certain that I wasn't dreaming. After some tests were carried out, it was confirmed: I was going to become a father! It was a surreal moment, I think. Amidst all of the problems I was trying to control, something joyous surfaced. Most people would probably say it was the best moment of their lives, but for me, it felt like something good had happened, but not overwhelmingly good. Perhaps it was the stress I had thrown upon me with Samantha's arrival or the fact that I was losing the plot, but finding out that I was going to become a father was more surrealistic than blissful.

When we returned to the flat after visiting the local doctor, Samantha told me off. She wasn't happy being alone. She didn't know how to speak French, so she couldn't communicate with anyone. And now she was pregnant, she needed someone to be with her all the time. The list went on, but there was nothing I could do. I knew I was the person to blame; I'd allowed myself to get into this position, but I only wished I could tell her why so she could understand. I wanted to be free as well, because I felt like a man shackled by the chains of a secret. I thought of a way to rid myself of the shackles and so I asked Samantha a question.

'Don't you think you should maybe look into my faith a little? You never know, it might interest you.'

'How?'

There were a lot of things that she had to learn and I knew it would take a lot of work before she accepted my faith, but I was glad she was willing to give it a try.

'I will speak to my friend Jibè, but you've got to pretend like there is nothing between us.'

To learn about the faith and devote yourself to God was like going to school again. You would be taught by a qualified pious person who would progressively recommend you for baptism if they felt you were spiritually ready. Depending on your ability to learn and willingness to change, the amount of time it would take to accept the teachings varied depending on the person. After asking me what learning my faith involved, I explained to Samantha that it involved helping people who wanted to get closer to God, study about his word, and cultivate a new way of life that differed from their past. She didn't respond to what I said. I thought that she may have refused my proposal, and noticing she was about to respond, I interrupted.

'You won't be forced to accept the faith, but you will be helped to make a choice.'

She didn't respond.

My behaviour at Mama Cathy's home became increasingly suspicious. Some days, I'd leave home at 1am and wouldn't return until late at night. Other days, I'd return home at 2am. I simply didn't want anything I'd later regret to happen to Samantha. Sometimes, Matthew would have to make up a story for me to tell Mama Cathy why I wasn't home. But I didn't know how long all of this acting could last. I was getting more fatigued, and with little sleep, it was difficult to keep on going. The look on Mama Cathy's face told me that she knew I was hiding something from her. Perhaps, she was waiting for the right time to catch me out when I least expected.

Meanwhile, I had set up an arrangement for Jibè to be visiting Samantha and teach her about my faith. I was always nervous when Jibè was around and was always with him when he was with Samantha. I was also there as a translator, since Samantha couldn't speak French. I didn't want anyone to find out a thing. One day, after Jibè had finished his lesson, he spoke to me.

'Who's that girl?'

'She's just a girl I met that said she wanted to get closer to God.'

'That's funny. Remember, some time ago you told me about a girl called Samantha and you showed me her picture? That looks like her.'

'I don't know what you're talking about.'

'That picture, it had a girl who looks like her. You showed me that day, that you were interested in her.'

'Oh! No, no, no, no,' I hurriedly replied.

'Oh right, she just looks exactly like her.'

'Yeah, that's funny how people can look alike,' I continued. 'So what do you have planned later for today?'

I managed to avoid any further questions on Samantha, but I was nearly found out. That was too close!

Samantha was now over four months pregnant. The tension at home was also beginning to rise. Mama Cathy was beginning to wonder why I wasn't staying at home. Jibè also began to suspect that I was hiding something from him. My health was dwindling and I could see the desperation on Samantha's face, as she didn't want anything to happen to me, especially since I was the only person she knew in Gabon.

I didn't want Mama Cathy to find out about Samantha, and so I convinced Samantha to move to another place, which was about a further mile from where she currently resided. We moved to a place called *Sodico*. It was in the suburbs of Libreville and it would be difficult for anyone to locate us there. I thought it would help lower suspicions, but I had no idea.

Two months after we moved to Sodico, one night, Samantha complained of stomach cramps. I thought it was just regular stomach pain, and thought it would get better. Perhaps we should've been on our way to see Dr Ndjendje, the doctor at the local private clinic, but it was too late at night. I'd been having sleepless nights so I took the opportunity to monitor how she was feeling. She was able to sleep in the early hours of the morning, and I left her asleep. I decided to return to Mama Cathy's place so that she wouldn't realise that I was not at home for the entire night. I woke up at 8am and Mama Cathy hadn't suspected that I'd left. It was a normal day, and nothing seemed to interrupt the balance. As usual, I was at the block factory with Matthew where I would set everyone to work, before I would leave to see Samantha. I wanted to see if she was okay after her stomach cramps, and was in a hurry to also get some much needed sleep.

As I began to leave the block factory, I saw Ade coming towards me. Ade was our next door neighbour at Sodico and I wondered what brought him near my factory.

'Ade! Ade!' I shouted.

'Oh Peter, thank God I still found you here!'

'Why? What happened?'

'It's Samantha. She needs you now and it's urgent.'

The landlord's wife had been left with Samantha, while Ade came looking for me.

Hearing the anxiety in Ade's voice, I rushed home. I found Samantha in a pool of blood. Her crimson-like blood was spread all over the floor. Her body was being held up by the landlord's wife. My heart skipped a beat.

'Samantha!' I screamed.

She wouldn't speak or open her eyes. I didn't know what to do. I approached her, tapping her face, searching for a response. Anything to prove she was still alive.

'What happened?' I asked the landlord's wife.

'She couldn't…'

'She couldn't what?' Speak to me,' I yelled desperately.

The landlord's wife began to cry in panic. I knelt down and began to tap Samantha's face again.

'Wake up Samantha! Don't do this to me. Wake up!'

As I tapped her face continuously, she slowly opened her eyes.

'Samantha!'

A surge of relief overwhelmed me.

Samantha had miscarried. She was so weak and tired. We quickly called a taxi. Meanwhile, I called Dr Ndjendje to expect our arrival. As we drove in the taxi, she screamed uncontrollably and was writhing in pain. I only hoped she could forgive me for what I'd made her go through. I knew if anything happened to her my life was over. We hurried the taxi as we made our way to *Centre Médical de Nzeng-Ayong*. When we arrived at the medical centre, she was rushed into the emergency room. After a few hours, she was transferred to a general hospital closer to the centre of Libreville. The pain she must've been going through was unbearable to hear, let alone to watch her experience. She was operated on at the hospital and then discharged that night. I couldn't explain why they'd let her go so soon. She was not in the physical condition to go home. Yet, my complaints yielded no mercy. She was simply given medications to ease the pain and we were advised to purchase other drugs so she could continue her treatment at home.

It was truly one of the saddest moments of our lives. Samantha barely survived the ordeal. She'd just lost a six month pregnancy. It would have been our first child; I would have been a father. It was then that it just hit me, what we could have had and what we lost. Ade and I took Samantha home. While Ade kept her in company, I went to the pharmacy to purchase the drugs Samantha desperately needed. Ogbonnaya, one of my Nigerian friends, decided to follow me realising that I was in distress.

We took a bus to Carreffour Iai from Sodico and stopped off at a large roundabout where most taxis and buses normally made a U-turn. We then took another bus to Belleville. There was no space in the bus, and we didn't know when the next bus would arrive. As a result, I decided to take the first bus while Ogbonnaya would take the next one that came. We would then meet up later on. As we travelled the roads, I saw the military barracks ahead, and the cemetery on my right. We were heading for a left turn, when suddenly, a lorry driver had lost control of his lorry. He was spiralling and moving at our bus with great speed. There wasn't a second to think about anything. Everyone on the bus began to scream and shout.

'Stop! Stop!'

We were going to make a direct collision. There were only seconds spare. I couldn't move because we were packed so tightly in the bus. I looked above. The lorry driver had tried to apply his brakes and the bus driver was doing the same, but the collision could not be averted. Lives were going to be lost. While the bus driver grappled for control of his vehicle, we began to spiral. It was either I got out or I would die.

Impact. Everything happened in slow motion. I'm sitting in the second row of the bus. There are passengers in the row ahead of me and the row behind. Everyone is screaming. I see a small gap open in the sliding doors. I reach for the handle, wrench the door open and jump through. As I do so, a stridency of sound hits my ears like a tidal wave. The harsh, crunching metal grates the ground, as I hear the tinkling of glass when it shatters. Small flames begin to rise from the bus. There's so much noise. I land on the floor in agony and pain. I feel lightheaded and my vision begins to fade, but I'm still awake; I'm still listening. Then I hear people scream, until suddenly everything goes dark.

I woke up at the hospital. I tried to get up, but I couldn't. Surprisingly, I didn't feel any pain. I saw my wrists attached to an intravenous drip, and my legs had a long cast. I saw Ogbonnaya sitting on a chair a few metres away and as I began to engage my brain as to what was happening, I got a huge punch in my temple — headache.

'What happened?' I dazedly asked

'Oh my goodness, you're awake. Thank God!'

'What happened?'

'I'll tell you later. You need to rest.'

'What about Samantha?'

'She's fine and Mama Cathy's on her way. Don't worry, just rest.'

'I've got to go.'

I try to get up, but get punched again and yell in pain.

'Just rest Peter, don't worry.'

A few hours later, I feel better enough to talk. I was told five people died and it was a fatal accident. Most people had lost limbs. I was fortunate to still have my feet the doctor told me. Ogbonnaya still hadn't got the drugs for Samantha. I told him to go and tell Samantha what had happened. I got Ogbonnaya to help me write a note to give to her. I knew she would be worried, but there was nothing more I could do.

After Ogbonnaya left, Mama Cathy arrived about an hour later. She was devastated to see me in my condition. Apparently, news had spread in the area of the crash. Mama Cathy asked why I was in the bus at that time, but I couldn't disclose the full account of what had actually happened. I simply told her that I was going to pick up a few things.

A few days later, I was discharged from hospital with crutches. I was also assigned a physiotherapist who would massage my foot at home. I was worried that I couldn't see Samantha, but hoped that I would get better quickly. Matthew and my other friends helped to transmit messages between Samantha and myself. It was difficult, but manageable. Most people thought that I would be on crutches for the rest of my life. No one saw it feasible that I would be able to walk again. But after a month, I began to start walking again gradually. It was a surprise to me, let alone others, that I could walk. At first, I was just happy to survive the incident, but with the improvements I was making, I would be able to walk again.

Weeks later, things got back to a relatively normal level. But things got so bad at Sodico that we had to move away. We found accommodation in Owendo around March 1997. Owendo was a port city in Gabon and a south-west suburb of Libreville. The accommodation was largely surrounded with high-rising vegetation. It was even further away from Sodico and it was always quiet in the area. It was a perfect hide out, but for Samantha, a prison. She soon got pregnant again, but life was generally poor. The loneliness and stress she underwent was overwhelming. Since the miscarriage, she didn't want to carry on with lessons about my faith and felt it bored her. She was getting fed up with me and was urging me to move her away from where she was. I wasn't happy with the conditions either, but what could I do? I had to protect my secret. Frankly, I was fed up; I was at tipping point. But I could do nothing.

As time passed, our arguments became a common thing, but I had to be careful because she was pregnant. Her main complaint was her isolation, the fact she had no one to speak to when I wasn't there. And I could understand that completely. But at that moment, I was facing one of the biggest challenges of my life. I was keeping a secret, and the consequences of anyone finding out, would be greater than my present situation actually being a secret. My business wasn't doing well either, as I spent most of my time trying to please everyone else. It had been over a year since our introduction, and nobody knew where we were. Essentially, Samantha hadn't spoken to her family since she arrived from England, and I hadn't spoken to mine since my introduction. I knew Mary would have been worried.

'I don't want to have my baby in this forest. Get me out of here!'

Samantha had begun to cry again. I felt embarrassed and ashamed for myself. I couldn't take the crying, the running around and the sleepless nights anymore. It was breaking me. On the outside I looked calm, but inside I was screaming and yelling for direction.

Six months later, the situation had still not changed. One day, I arrived very late at the block factory from Owendo. I was exhausted after spending most of the day with Samantha, and I went to the factory to find out about the sales of the day. As I went to sit down, Matthew approached me.

'Hi bro.'

'Hi Matthew. How are you?'

'I'm fine, Jibè is over there,' Matthew said pointing at the restaurant. 'He's been waiting for you for a few hours.'

Surprised and also shattered, I saw Jibè sitting in the corner at the restaurant.

'Hi Peter!'

'Hi Jibè.'

'You good?'

'Yeah, I'm actually busy right now. I was just going to find out the sales for today and then make my way home.'

'You're always on your way somewhere,' he continued. 'I've been waiting here for nearly the whole day so that I would see you.'

'Oh, I'm sorry. I've just been busy.'

'I don't even see you anymore Peter. Where have you been?'

'You know, around somewhere.'

'Where?'

'I don't even know. Erm, did you need me?'

'Peter, what is going on with you?'

'Nothing Jibè, I'm fine. Look.'

I jumped up and down and smiled.

'You're losing weight, Mama Cathy tells me you don't stay at home, your business is on the verge of collapse, and I rarely see you anymore. Peter, what's your problem?'

I didn't reply. I began thinking about whether to tell Jibè when I didn't realise that I was pensive in front of him.

'Peter,' Jibè yelled. 'Talk to me. I'm meant to be your friend.'

After much persuasion, I told Jibè everything. It was hard for me to tell him. Sometimes, I would just stop as I recounted the experience. Once I finished, Jibè consoled me and advised me to speak with Fefe about the matter. After telling Jibè my situation, it felt like a huge weight was lifted off my shoulders. I think it was sheer desperation and fatigue that pushed me over the edge. I was dying and when Jibè extended his hand, I took a firm hold.

A week later, I spoke to Fefe about what I had done. I was expressly nervous beforehand, but I had to tell him.

'You mean to say that you're married and your wife is pregnant!'

'Yes.'

After narrating the whole account, Fefe was astonished. Fefe knew what I had experienced at the hands of Mama Cathy because of Jessica as well as Jean because of M'bembi, so there was a little sympathy and pity from Fefe as I told the story. Immediately after my visit to Fefe, a meeting was arranged to meet Mama Cathy. Fefe and Jibè would accompany me to visit Mama Cathy to discuss the matter. To say that I was scared, frightened or afraid were all mediocre adjectives compared to what I was actually feeling. I was about to tell Mama Cathy what I had done. Fefe and Jibè gave me courage, but even a lion would have cowered in front of Mama Cathy when it came to an issue like this.

Fefe called Mama Cathy to sit down in the living room.

'What is going on?' Mama Cathy asked, looking at Fefe, Jibè and me.

'We are here to see you Mama. Peter has something important to tell you,' Fefe replied.

'I'm sorry. I was scared with the way Jessica's matter was going on and on. The person I really wanted was M'bembi. But I was denied her love because her father claimed I was Nigerian.'

Surprised at what was going on, Mama Cathy looked at me in puzzled fashion. I continued.

'So while all of this was going on, I went to the registry and got married. Her parents weren't aware of it, because they refused to let us do it,' I hurriedly said.

'You've gotten married!! To who? M'bembi?'

'No, a woman called Samantha who I met in Nigeria.'

'WHAT?! WHEN?! HOW?!'

Mama Cathy was an epitome of anger. Realising that she had shouted me into silence, she calmed down and asked me another question.

'So for how long have you been together?'

'We got married in November 1994, and she's now six months pregnant.'

Mama Cathy was about to hit the roof with her temper, but calmed it down again after hearing she was pregnant.

'Why did you hide it from me?'

'I didn't know how you'd react and when you were always talking about Jessica, I didn't know what to do.'

The tension in the conversation rose and we were all waiting patiently for Mama Cathy's response.

'You shouldn't have hid the matter from me even if you know I'll be angry. Where is Samantha now?'

Before I could reply, Fefe interrupted.

'All we want is your approval. We will arrange for her arrival.'

'Although I am very angry Peter, you are my son, so please bring my daughter home. And as a little sorry gift to me you will name him after my father, Arouna Ndjom.'

Surprisingly, after her fits of anger, Mama Cathy was excited with the news that she was to be a grandmother. Fefe and Jibè were especially surprised with her reaction.

'Now that all is well,' Fefe said. 'We will arrange for Samantha to arrive.'

Soon after, the meeting ended. The chains of the secret had been released from my hands and I couldn't have felt happier. To feel free in my heart was incredible. Mama Cathy began to announce to her neighbours that I had gotten married and my wife was arriving soon. She then arranged a party for Samantha and me. When I told Samantha what had happened, she was so happy.

'I'd been waiting for this day.'

Finally, we could live a somewhat more settled life. A few days later, she arrived at Mama Cathy's place. Mama Cathy had arranged a huge welcoming party and the sense of joy you got from being there was unbelievable. People treated Samantha like they had known her all her life. The warmth and love she received was incredible. News soon spread amongst my friends that I had a wife, and Mama Cathy warmly accepted Samantha into the family. It was remarkable to see Mama Cathy embracing Samantha and joking around with her. I always knew that Mama Cathy would be the hardest person to convince, yet I was proved so enthrallingly wrong. I guess people are unpredictable and you never really know what people think until you ask. You always learn something new every day…

Me (centre) weightlifting with the general public in Libreville

Tom (left to right), me, Arouna and Eko in 2007

Kate's younger sister (back), Kate's mother (front, left) and Kate (front, right)

Kate's older sister (left) and Kate (right)

Kate (left) with relative (right)

Fefe (right) teaching me about the creed (left)

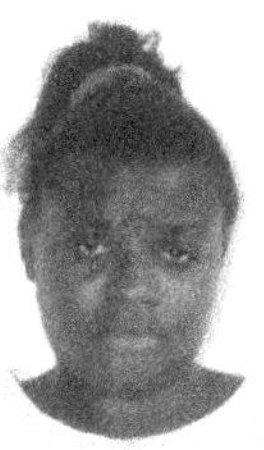
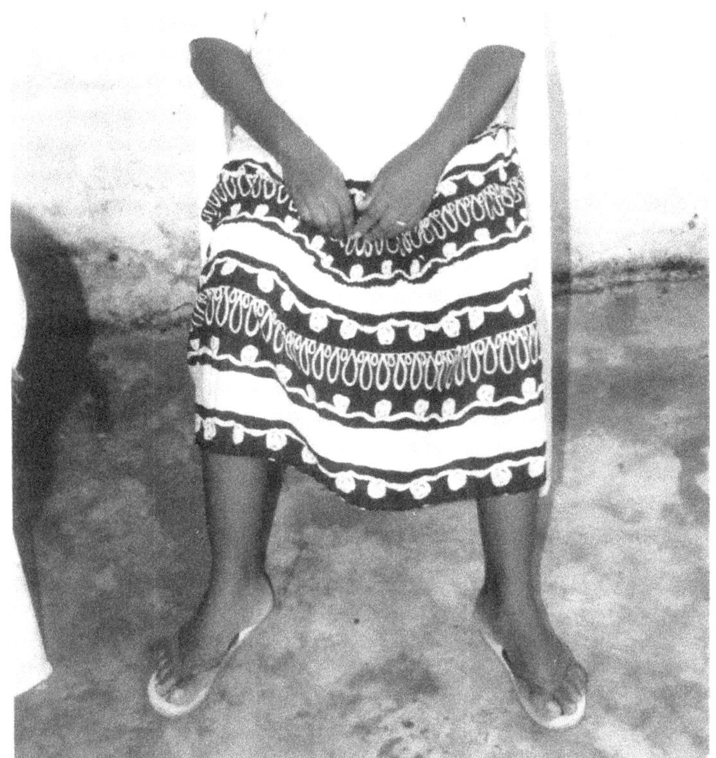

Samantha in 1996

Chapter 19: Forced to Walk

Hearing the first cry Arouna made brought chills down my spine. In the early hours of that lukewarm December morning in 1997, Samantha gave birth to our first child. I was euphoric, but Mama Cathy looked even more so. She was dancing and running around the house with such happiness; it was great to see. It'd been quite a while since I'd heard from Mary and I received no news of her. Palpably, she would have been worried. After Arouna was born, I sent a letter to Mary and Samantha's parents. I just hoped they would receive it.

A month after Arouna's birth, I received a notice from the Gabonese authorities:

ATTENTION!
VOTRE BÂTIMENT SERA DÉMOLI. VOUS AVEZ DEUX SEMAINES POUR QUITTER LES LIEUX.

ATTENTION!
YOUR BUILDING WILL BE DEMOLISHED. YOU HAVE TWO WEEKS TO VACATE THE PREMISES.

I couldn't believe what was happening. Why was the block factory and restaurant being demolished? I searched around the neighbourhood if anyone could give me answers and each building I passed, they too had received notice from the government. The Gabonese government was repossessing people's land and my building was listed. No one understood why the government was carrying out such action. I was paralysed with shock; what could I possibly do? Apparently, the decision to knock down our buildings had been made months ago, what meaningful thing could I do to stop it? Two weeks later, men in their bulldozers came. I watched as these men brought down my business to ruins — literally. All I had worked so hard to achieve for a number of years, the business that gave me a source of income, and the work I did to keep me off the streets was gone only in a matter of seconds. So it hit me: Rome wasn't built in one day, but it could be destroyed in one instant. I thought about walking in front of the bulldozers to stop them from tearing down my livelihood, but there were gendarmes guarding the entire area. One step closer to my building and I would have been taken to a police station.

I couldn't understand why the authorities were being so harsh. Perhaps the worst thing was hearing news that others in a similar situation had been given compensation.

For the moment, my major concern was how I was going to take care of Samantha and Arouna without a job. After having considered the impact that my joblessness would have on our family, we decided it would be better for Samantha to return to England with Arouna and stay with her sister. At least in England, they would both be taken care of and that would allow me the time to sort out my life. But it wasn't an easy task separating Mama Cathy from Arouna. Mama Cathy had become Arouna's personal nurse. Samantha and I hardly touched him for three months, as he was always in the arms of Mama Cathy. She insisted that Samantha stayed in Gabon. Mama Cathy loved us dearly and offered to help provide for our needs until I was able to find a job, but we couldn't take it. We had to help ourselves; we couldn't rely on Mama Cathy all the time. Samantha and Arouna had to return to England. We didn't know whether it would be a good idea, but it was the best option we had.

In April 1998, Samantha and Arouna would leave to Gabon for England. It was really tough for Mama Cathy, as she cried all the way to the airport.

'Why are you separating my child from me?' she repeatedly asked.

'Mama, I promise you will see them soon again. It's just for a small period of time, until I put myself together again.'

I never planned for Samantha and Arouna to leave and it was hitting me pretty hard too. In one day, my business was destroyed. After years of building it, it took one day to bring it down. So I guess being alone for some time would also help me refocus and think about my next actions.

'Papa, make sure you come to look for me one day.'

Arouna smiled. Mama Cathy always called Arouna 'Papa' and it was so moving to see her in the mood she was. Samantha was somewhat happy to be leaving Gabon, and was eagerly anticipating the day she would leave. She had a huge smile on her face and didn't look too upset to be leaving. Perhaps after all she'd gone through, it was understandable. She passed through immigration and waved one final goodbye to Mama Cathy and me.

'Have a good trip!' I shouted.

'Bye! Bye!' Mama Cathy added.

Would Samantha really visit Mama Cathy and me in Gabon again? I wasn't really too sure. But for now, I was determined to place my life back on track.

A few days after Samantha had left with Arouna, I began to find out why the government was not repossessing my land, as I was led to believe at first. After speaking to a few people, I soon understood they had just decided to demolish a few buildings for the sake of it. Realising that this had happened, I couldn't believe how invidious the Gabonese authorities could be. How could they be so spiteful?

Thankfully, I still had a little amount of money left over from the profits of the block factory that I had saved up. After speaking with my friend James, who sold building materials in his shop, I decided to start up a carwash business. The land, which ostensibly belonged to the government, was still available, so I used it to station my carwash. I had a little experience of working at a carwash, so I employed a few people, bought a few resources and began to get my place running again. I asked Eko if he was interested in working with me, and he agreed. He soon became my supervisor. Although it wasn't business as usual, my carwash business began to grow and I was making some money again.

During this time, I occasionally helped James at his workshop. But two months progressed and I realised that there was nothing really worthwhile working for. Even though I had my carwash, it wasn't making as much money as my block factory did, and I didn't know whether the government would be back again to knock it down. I spoke to James about it, and for once it seemed like there might be a way. I knew that I could restart my trade business, which was profitable for me a few years back. I remembered how Mr Kalu would travel overseas to buy goods, and then return to sell them in Gabon. I wanted to do the same thing, as I knew it would make me a lot of money quickly. Perhaps I could also rebuild my business.

When I spoke to James about my intentions, he offered his help. He told me how the spare car parts business was profitable in Gabon, and a lucrative business venture. After thinking about it, I decided to give it a try. James then spoke to his brother Martin, who lived in Germany. Telling him I wanted to get involved in the spare car parts business, Martin sent me an invitation letter to visit Germany. I was completely astounded by his kindness; it was just too good to be true. All of sudden, I would be travelling to a European country. I thought I would never be able to buy and sell goods on the same scale as Mr Kalu, so it brought huge joy to me when I received the invitation. I knew this would be a great opportunity to begin my trade business again. I would use the little funds I had to build the business again. I was given a two month visa and quickly arranged my ticket details. I would be on transit in Morocco, and that would give me a great chance to see a little of Morocco. These were places I never thought I'd visit in my life, so it was simply overwhelming to be in that position.

I wished that I could visit Samantha in the UK, but no one was interested in inviting me. It was something that I could understand, yet not at the same time. Regardless, I was really looking forward to visiting Morocco and Germany. When Mama Cathy found out that I would be travelling, she was also very happy for me. Mama Cathy and my friends arranged a meal before I left and we certainly had an entertaining evening. The following day, I was on my way to Leon M'ba International Airport with the happiness within my heart causing a bounce in my feet.

Within a few hours, we were in the sky. Several hours later, we arrived at Casablanca Mohammed V Airport, where we would be on transit. I lodged myself into one of the beachside hotels near the airport and took a few pictures. The following morning, I boarded my flight to Hamburg International Airport.

I arrived in Hamburg in the late evening of that day and I decided to give Samantha a call.

'Hi Samantha. It's me Peter.'

'Peter? Where are you?' she said astonished. 'This is a German telephone code.'

'Yes, I'm in Hamburg at the moment.'

'Hamburg! How did you get there?'

'My friend invited me. I don't know how it happened, but it did.'

'Why didn't you tell me?'

'I know, I know. I should have. But I didn't want to burden you with anything. And I wanted it to be a surprise.'

Hamburg was a beautiful city, but was equally very busy. I had arrived in the warm summer of June 1998. Hearing the German language, walking on the large streets, travelling on the trams around the city, seeing the smiles and waves of people as they took boat trips on the glistening rivers of Hamburg and walking past the bakery shop on the way home just to smell the freshly baked bread — Hamburg was truly worth the wait.

I stayed at Martin's place and helped him with the motor parts business. Meanwhile, I was also carrying out my goods trades. The days went by quite quickly and I was beginning to get comfortable living in Germany. There was just over a month left on my visa when I felt it was perhaps good to see Samantha and Arouna before I returned to Gabon. I thought the best way to see them is for them to come over. A few days later, I travelled to Essen with one of my friends. We had gone to purchase some parts. Meanwhile, I called Samantha.

'Hello Samantha.'

'Hi Peter.'

'How are you keeping?'

'I'm fine thanks, what about you? How's Hamburg?'

'It's good. It's good. The business is going quite well and I'm surviving let's say.'

'That's great.'

'You know, I was just wondering…you know, whether you would like to visit me in Germany. We could go sightseeing with Arouna, we could travel a bit, we'd be able to see each other again. What d'you think?'

'I think it's a great idea, but I don't have any money to get a ticket and I don't suppose you do. I'm not working. At the end of the day, my sister and her husband have been taking care of Arouna and me. I just don't know if it'll be possible.'

'I understand. That's why I'm prepared to send you the ticket money.'

'What? You can do that?'

'Yes, yes. I'll send you the money and you can make your way to Essen.'

'Essen? I thought you stayed in Hamburg.'

'Oh yeah, I forgot. I'm staying in Essen for a while now. I needed to get some spare parts, but one of my friends has also taken me in. The place is alright and my friend is okay with you and Arouna coming over…So why not?'

Within a few days, she and Arouna arrived in Essen to see me. Everything happened so quickly, but I was glad to see them both, especially Arouna who was now six months old. It was great to see my family together again.

It'd now been three weeks since Samantha arrived in Essen. My visa would soon be expiring and Samantha and Arouna would soon have to return to England. Meanwhile, we'd made quite a number of friends while staying in Germany. I'd met Francis and Singh in Dussern at a gathering. Francis, who came from Nigeria, lived in Düsseldorf, while Singh, an Indian man, stayed in Duisburg. We practiced the same faith, so it was easier to begin a friendly rapport. Although Samantha still didn't practice the same faith, we had met so many new friends through Francis and Singh. I also became very close to Ugochukwu Anyanwu, or who we all nicknamed: Hugo. He came from Nigeria also. When we first arrived in Essen, he would take us sightseeing and settled us down completely. It was great having him around.

I only had a few days left in Germany and I had already made a lot of new friends. In fact, I didn't want to go anymore. Life felt a lot better than it had in Gabon, and I almost forgot that I had come to Germany for business. At finding this out, Singh sought legal advice on my situation, perhaps to find any way to extend my stay in Germany. In no time, Singh managed to arrange a meeting with a woman named Andrea. She was a lawyer that specialised in immigration. She was extremely friendly and told me what had to happen for me to continue to stay in Germany.

'The only condition for you to lengthen your stay in Germany is that your wife must have a job, you must have a place to live and then we have to hope that the Bundesrepublik Deutschland...erm... German state gives you a permit. But if not then you must leave Germany before your visa expires.'

Andrea then told us to visit the immigration office, presenting these documents and then hope that the state issues me a permit. But she let us know that nothing was guaranteed even if Samantha managed to get a job or we got a place of our own. And there wasn't much time left. Immediately after we left Andrea's office, Singh, Francis, me and all of our friends began to look for a job for Samantha. We spent days visiting various places and tendering in applications, but still we could get no response. We tried everything to get Samantha a job, but we couldn't. Eventually, after no success, we decided that Samantha would return to England, and I would have to return to Gabon. It was unfortunate that we'd already rented a two bedroom flat, and we'd have to give it up, but there was nothing more we could do. Everyone was upset and frustrated with the outcome, even Andrea tried her best to look for a job for Samantha. I simply had to accept that the very next day I would be making my way back to Gabon, while Samantha would return to England.

The following morning Samantha and I got dressed, knowing we would be heading our separate ways. For me it would be a return ticket to Gabon, for Samantha a one-way ticket to England. As we prepared to hand in our flat keys of where we stayed at 108 Blücherstraße in Duisburg to Singh who lived on the next street, Samantha received a call from Maredo restaurant in Königstraße to come to their office immediately. We were completely surprised at the news and decided to quickly hurry to the office. When we arrived at the manager's office, Samantha was congratulated instantly.

'Congratulations! You have got a job at Maredo. Your application has been accepted and this is your letter of employment.'

We couldn't believe our ears. Samantha was being given a job. This was exactly what we needed. Our joy and excitement was overwhelming. Singh had accompanied us also and the elation in his voice was indescribable. The manager, Chef Volker, was surprised at why we were so excited, and when we briefly explained what the job meant to us, he too was very happy for us. In a rush, we called Andrea on the phone and told her what happened.

'What are you calling me for? Hurry! Go! Get to the German immigration office now.'

Without delay, we rushed all the way to the German immigration office with Samantha's letter of employment. Beforehand, Andrea had already provided us any necessary documents that could help our case. She always told us to prepare to leave if we were not given the resident permit, as there was no guaranty and to make sure that I didn't overstay my visa so that I would be allowed to return to Germany. Bringing that advice back into my mind, Samantha and I waited patiently in the immigration building, before we were called in by an officer.

'Have you booked already a flight back to where you were coming from?'

'Yes,' I replied.

'That's good. You're very prepared for every eventuality.'

'Yes.'

'Well then Mr and Mrs…'

He looked at our faces and looked down at our passports, before pronouncing our surname.

'Sey-nu?'

I nodded.

'You're going to have to cancel your ticket. You will be staying in Germany for five years. Mrs Sey-nu, you will continue to work in Germany and Mr Sey-nu, you can also look for a job or start a business. Congratulations! You are now German residents.'

I began to thank the officers. I couldn't in any other way express my happiness. It was too good to be true. I remember at the immigration office where Mama Cathy took me, I thought no feeling could match what I experienced. Yet, this trumped it by a mile. I was now an official resident of Germany.

I knew Mama Cathy, Matthew and Eko would be expecting to pick me up at the airport the following day, so I called Mama Cathy and Matthew to tell them the news. Both of them were ecstatic. I rejoiced with them over the phone and I thanked Mama Cathy for everything she did for me. For now, I was not returning to Gabon, and the joy of staying in Germany overwhelmed me. The beautiful country I once knew had gone up a level; it was now the miracle country.

Life in Germany was turning out to be great. Samantha had started work, while I stayed behind to look after Arouna. He was a handsome young boy; people always said he took after his mother. A few weeks after I'd been granted my permit, I thought about returning back to education. I sent a letter to the correspondent school I found when I was in Gabon, and wondered whether I could use the time I had now to finish the courses I had abandoned. My educational ambition grew, especially when I always held the promise I had made to Mary in the back of my mind.

It'd been two years since I'd seen Mary and I felt very upset that I had not gone and seen her yet. Despite the number of letters I sent, she hadn't replied, which was extremely unusual. I couldn't wait to tell her that I had now moved to Germany and I was rekindling my dream of getting back to school. I missed Mary dearly, but I was also beginning to miss Mama Cathy too. I didn't know where my journey was taking me, but I had left everything behind me now. Even though I looked ahead, there were still people I loved dearly that were part of my past. Would I ever see Lemmy or Robert again? Would I see Kate? What about Texan, Yanke, Matthew and Kofi? Would I return to Gabon? There were serious questions to ponder on, but for now, I was enjoying every moment of being an official resident of Europe. I guess running away on the ship wasn't so much of a bad idea, or was it?

Chapter 20: Her Legacy

Two years passed. Samantha, Arouna and I had really begun to settle down in Germany. Being 30 years old with no real qualifications, it was difficult to find a job in Germany. Nevertheless, after searching for so long, I found a job in *Albert's Restaurant* in Oberhausen, which was located between Duisburg and Essen. Hugo also worked at Albert's Restaurant and had petitioned his manager, if they could offer me a job. My abilities were placed in the kitchen, where I worked as a dishwasher.

Working at Albert's Restaurant was always fun. Although the job title 'dishwasher' made it seem like I had a menial task, the happiness, laughter and jokes in the kitchen usually caused a ruckus for the manager. Since Hugo and I went to work together, he always reminded me not to be late. We started work at 5pm and closed at 11pm. When coming home, I had to make sure I didn't miss the last train travelling towards Duisburg or else I couldn't get home. Hugo and I had a great time working at Albert's Restaurant.

Later that year, in August 2000, I managed to find a way to speak with Vincent. After finding a number of his in-law and speaking to them, I was able to find out Vincent's new number. The last time I'd spoken to him was at the introduction of Samantha and I, which was more than four years ago. I hadn't been able to tell anyone back home that I was now living in Germany and it almost felt like time was flying by. Happy that I finally had his number, I called him.

'Hello Vincent, it's me Peter.'

'Peter?'

'Yes, it's me.'

'Who?'

'Peter, Peter,' I continued. 'Brother, how are you?'

'Peter…so after all this time you couldn't even call home.'

'I'm sorry. I've just been tied up with a lot of things.'

There was a pause.

'How are you though brother?'

'Four years Peter. Four years, you couldn't even give me a call. I looked for your number from everyone I knew — every number failed. What's going on?'

'I'm sorry Vincent. It's just that a lot of things have happened in the last few years.'

'Where are you?'

'I'm in Germany at the moment.'

'Germany? How did you get there?'

'It's a long story, but I'll tell you later.'

'How's Samantha and your son?'

'They're both well.'

'I'm glad that you called anyway. It's good to hear your voice again.'

'It's good to hear yours too brother,' I continued. 'How's Mary, Tony and the rest of the family?'

'Yeah, Tony and the rest of the family are fine.'

'What about Mary?'

'That's one of the reasons why I wanted to call you…a few things have happened since you left Nigeria.'

'Like what?'

'I want you to take heart with what I'm about to say.'

'Is Mary sick? Is she okay? Have people hurt her?...'

'Peter, Peter. Stop. I really want you to take heart with what I'm about to tell you.'

'Vincent, what's happened?'

'I want you to be strong.'

'Vincent! What's happened?!'

'Mary's dead.'

My life collapsed in front of me. My heart broke out of my chest as I screamed at the top of my voice. Then, I was hit by a deafening silence. Pain began to flow down my cheeks, as I began to swell in my emotions and my lips quivered. Paralysed by what I'd heard, I sat there with the phone at my ear and stared at the walls, rocking back and forth on my chair. Vincent was saying something, but I had blocked him out. I felt weak, tired and apathetic. As more tears came, the regular adrenaline rushes in my heart were causing me discomfort. It was a heartrending, poignant moment. Every feeling and emotion I had felt with Mary punched and bruised my head. Mary was reason why I tried so hard every day — to help her in the same way she had helped me. And now I couldn't, because she was dead.

Vincent's shouting brought me out of my trance.

'Peter, talk to me. Peter! Peter!'

'Yes.'

My body shook and convulsed, as if I had no control over it. I struggled to breathe with each desperate gasp of air I took, only to release it again in another forceful sob.

'Peter, I need you to listen to me.'

'It's over Vincent,' I said, my voice trembling.

'No it's not.'

'She's gone.'

'She's never gone Peter. She'll always be in your heart and mind.'

'It's my fault.'

'Peter, you're not the one to blame. She got ill, died a few days later and she got buried. Sometimes things like this happen Peter…she was old.'

'I should have gone and visited her,' the agitation in my voice was growing.

'Peter, this is not your fault.'

'I wasn't there when she needed me…and now she's dead,' my voice trailed off until my flooded eyes could hold back no more tears.

'Peter, I'm so sorry. I need to go now, something's happened. I'm sorry.'

'It's fine.'

Before Vincent continued, I ended the call.

Mary had left me alone to suffer in the cruel world. For several hours, I sat by myself, withdrawn from the world, and cried. Mary had been a stronghold in my life. I wanted her to be alive to see me fulfil my promise. I wanted to tell her that I'd made it to Germany. I wanted to tell her that I was getting back to school. I wanted to tell her that I was going to visit her. I wanted to tell her one last time before her eyes closed on the world that I loved her. But I couldn't…I couldn't believe that she had died simply from a natural illness. There was something wrong. Mary couldn't die now; it was impossible. She needed to see my son. She needed to be there when I graduated from university. She needed to just be alive. I just needed to see her one last time…

Once I had put myself together somewhat, I called Mama Cathy and Matthew to tell them about the news. Astounded and upset, they both offered me their sincere condolences.

A month later, I made my way to Nigeria. On the day I arrived, I went to where Mary was buried. She was buried in front of her house. That day, I investigated everything that had happened before she died. The results were shocking. Mary was called all sorts of vile names, sworn at and insulted publicly. Vincent had told me that Mary had gotten ill; instead, I was told she died of hunger. But I began to think that that was impossible, especially since I remember having given Mary a lot of money. I was told that she was left to live in solitude. While these stories were being narrated, Vincent and some of Beki's children had accompanied me. As I looked at their faces, their guilt was written on their foreheads.

Vincent's wife had been influenced by the rumours that the death of her first son was caused by Mary. Vincent and her wife both claimed she was a witch. It revolted me that they were frightened to visit Mary in the village because they thought she would eat them up. My anger grew with each person we spoke to and now I was obligated to find out more about her death, because as far as I was concerned Mary didn't die of a natural illness. As my curiosity increased, I went to visit Tony. As I walked through the door, he spoke almost immediately.

'Did they tell you she was a witch? Don't listen to them. It's all a lie. My sister is not a witch.'

I was glad to hear what Tony had said.

'Hi Papa.'

'Payoyo?'

'Yes, papa.'

'So it's you that has come through the door.'

'Yes, papa.'

'I thought you were another one of those villagers who had come to tell me that I was a fool for not believing my sister was a witch.'

Tony explained everything that had happened since my departure. Apparently, he had sent my half-brothers and sisters to check up on Mary in the village. But I didn't know whether to believe what he had said or not, especially when I'd heard from others she'd been left on her own.

I couldn't imagine how Mary must've felt in her last days — abandoned, dejected, worried, scared perhaps. What must've she been thinking when she was passing away. Imagine labouring your entire life to taking care of vulnerable, abandoned children and then in the few weeks before you die you are rewarded with revolting names. Was that fair? As days passed, it became clear that Mary's death was becoming a conspiracy. In fact, she hadn't just got ill — someone was responsible for her death. It just didn't make sense to me that she just got ill and died. Why did no one give her medical attention, especially if Tony had sent his children to see her? How did people know she had gotten ill? Was there an autopsy? Was there a coroner's report?

Mary's uncle's child was Sunny, and his wife Sedi had found Mary lying ill in her room. She then had given her medication to drink and food to eat. But it was said that she never returned to see Mary until she had died. Bino was aware of Mary's condition, but no one had taken her to the hospital or informed Tony about it. A few days later, Mary was found dead. It was said that her body was found swollen and all over her floor was vomited blood and food. There were numerous stories of her death, some less dramatic than others, but I just didn't know what to believe.

Mary owned a piece of farming land about three miles away from where she lived. A few weeks after her death, her next door neighbour tried to claim Mary's belongings and her land, I was told. Her death was turning into a conspiracy. Was she poisoned? Was she killed to inherit her land? Or was it because she was a *witch*?

Mary's uncle's family on her mother's side, living opposite her, was the first to find her dead. To which they called the attention of Ogongo, a family member from Mary's father's side of the family. Mary was then buried outside her home, next to her mother who was buried years ago. I was told that no one informed Tony of Mary's burial until two weeks after. Vincent was also unaware until someone named Gbeleyi travelled to the city to break the news. Joy didn't also hear of Mary's death until months later. It was all very odd and disoriented.

Mary's home had been abandoned for a long time, and it was becoming decrepit by the day. Some of the structures had collapsed, her burial ground was untidy and the house had not been cleaned since her death so that it begun to smell of death itself. Tears brimmed in my eyes as what I saw only made me angrier. I decided to phone Joy.

'How could you allow it to happen?'

'What? Peter?'

'How could you not visit Mary?'

Joy and I held a lengthy conversation on the phone, as I explained everything that I had been told. Joy was shocked as I was to hear about the stories that led to Mary's death.

It had all gone downhill for Mary when I left Nigeria in 1996. Tai and Janet no longer lived with Mary as they had gotten married, so Tai was also surprised at hearing the death of Mary. Tai had even promised to buy clothes for Mary for her next visit to the village.

There were too many murky waters surrounding the death of Mary. It was like the truth had been covered up and time had been wasted deliberately before telling anyone of her death. I just wondered who killed Mary and when would I find out the truth about her death? As days passed, I knew it would take time for the wound in my heart to heal, but her legacy and my memory of her, no one will be able to steal.

I decided to do what I could to give Mary a more fitting burial. I took a cutlass and cut the high growing vegetation around her home and built memorial ground — a small garden — in her honour. While I was building the memorial ground, it was very rare for people to speak to me or look me in the eye.

It was unfortunate to hear that Sedi died a month after Mary did, or I would have been able to gather some information from her since she was the last person that saw Mary alive. Another problem was that after several attempts to refurbish Mary's place, Bino and his father Sunny wouldn't allow it to happen. They claimed Mary was a woman and thus she had no right to a legacy in her own house. I couldn't believe what I was hearing; they must've been joking, because there was no way I was going to let Mary's home stay in its decrepit state.

The exact date of Mary's death was unknown to me. No one could say when exactly she died and proved how neglected she was to the family. I was told about her death in August, but it was made to seem like she had died that year. Instead, after I carried out my own independent research, I found out, and later had it confirmed by Tai, that Mary had died sometime in November 1997. To not know the exact date of her death was harrowing. She was then buried on a Monday, a few days after she died, but there was no record of her death or burial anywhere.

If it hadn't been for Mary's love and care, I don't know where I would've been in my life. Would I have been alive? The only thing I had of Mary was the burial ground. She was a living example of a brave woman, who cared and loved vulnerable and abandoned children. The pain in my heart was great and I don't think anyone really appreciated the fact that Mary had died, except perhaps Tai. The nightmares I had were returning; I just hoped Mary could forgive me. I said I would visit her, but I didn't. Perhaps it was my fault; I should've gone to visit her. Perhaps I could've prevented it. But it was too late.

I would never know what really happened to Mary, what she was thinking when she took her last breath, how she looked when she died, what she was saying. But one day, I would find out. Before I left, I vowed to fulfil my promise I had made to Mary when I was only a small boy: *I promise I will return to school someday. I promise.* Mary was gone in the flesh, but my memories of her would always remain. Mary was never the Iron Lady, she was *The Lady*.

Life wasn't the same when I returned back to Germany. I had lost someone who meant the world to me, but perhaps it was important for me to move on, especially for my family. I guess I was given another purpose and another dream to achieve: the dream of education. As days advanced, I gradually moved on with my life. But the steps I was about to take next were significant in forming a new chapter in my life. Perhaps I felt I had to do it, or that it was better to do it, but there was no turning back from what I was about to do: I was looking to relocate to England with my family.

I had passed my driving test in August 2001, and my ambition to return to school was great. After doing a little research, I discovered that university was where mature individuals went back to school and that England had some of the most illustrious and well-taught universities in the world. I thought that coming to England would give me a better access to education and to fulfil my now lifelong dream. It was my ambition; my debt to Mary. I imagined how she would be behind me every step of the way, giving me encouragement as I went along. She would steer me into the right path and guide me. Her mellow face would smile; she would've been so proud. Some people went back to school so they could get a well-paid job, I was going back to school to fulfil my dreams and a promise.

Five months later, in February 2002, I prepared to make my journey from Duisburg to London — by car. One of my friends, Mr Oshiriboa, was a shipping agent at the time and advised me on the particular route to take. I would be taking a near 600km journey to the Queen's land. Telling our friends we were leaving was probably the hardest part of making the trip. We had made so many friends in Germany, but now we would be leaving them behind. Only a few years earlier, I had been looking for a way to stay in Germany...I guess time waits for no man.

The air was sharp like broken glass, so that as I walked towards my car I was pricked by the cold German weather. It was very early on Saturday morning, and as I looked at my watch, the time was 2am. I'd just come from Albert's restaurant. I thought it would perhaps be unfair not to say farewell before departing. After all, I had had an amazing time with them, and I knew one person would definitely be unhappy that I had not told them I was leaving: Hugo. The regret in the manager's face was immense; he didn't want me to go. My other friends didn't want me to leave either, but my decision had already been made. Some couldn't believe that I was travelling in the early hours of the following day. It was certainly a sad moment for us all, but they all wished me the best for the future.

Most people were still asleep while Samantha and I loaded our red Opel saloon car with our belongings the night before. The car was packed until it could be packed no more. There was hardly any space for a passenger to sit and my rear view mirror was out of use as our belongings were blocking the rear window. The windows were tinted so that most of the inside could not be seen, while Arouna was tightly squeezed in the middle of the back seats, beside our 18 inch television. I just hoped we weren't apprehended by the police as we made our way onto the road, particularly when I only had my wing mirrors to see what was happening behind me. The worst thing was I had only got my driver's license less than five months ago. This was definitely going to be one of the hardest journeys I would make. Mr Oshiriboa had given me a map and told me the major places where I had to be alert while driving.

I started the engine of the car and knew these would be our last moments in Germany. After saying a prayer, we began heading west towards Gutenbergstraße. We drove for an hour on a very quiet road before taking our first left onto Poststraße. In no time, we had soon got onto the A40 without encountering a problem. We then drove towards Venlo, before getting on to the route towards Antwerpen or Eersel. After some time, we took the wrong route, which Mr Oshiriboa had warned us about, but managed to find our way back and take the right route. After thinking that that would be the only issue we'd encounter on the journey, there was another one. I should've kept right and followed the signs to Oostende, but

I was on the left. There were so many cars; I wondered how I was going to be able to cross onto my right. Then, I saw a small opening. Immediately, I quickly swerved onto the E40. On an extremely busy motorway, I had taken a huge risk. Thankfully, everyone was okay. Soon after, we stopped to get some diesel and for toilet breaks. I tried to relax my nerves and refocus for the next part of my journey.

It was an easier journey, but at one point, I had to stop and ask for directions from motorists on the easiest way to get to Calais. The signs were also quite helpful and we soon arrived there. We were directed to park behind other vehicles. Samantha, Arouna and I came out of our red Opel saloon drive, and joined the queue to board the ship to Dover. When all our details were checked, we walked up the staircases and sat in the ship, ready to sail to England. I was exceedingly tired and so were Samantha and Arouna. After an hour of waiting, we set sail and tried to catch a little sleep on the boat.

We arrived in Dover at midday and were soon heading to London. We had driven for a while, but I was getting very tired, so Samantha made sure to keep close attention on the signs and what was happening on the motorway. Suddenly, we realised that we had taken the wrong route. Instead of making our way to Chingford, we were heading to Chelmsford. Figuring out a way to make a U-turn, a car suddenly came right alongside us and the driver began to shout.

'SWERVE TO YOUR RIGHT! I SAID SWERVE TO YOUR RIGHT NOW!'

I couldn't understand why the driver was telling us to swerve right onto his lane. When I tried to ask him, he sped up. Then as I looked at my wing mirrors, I knew what he was talking about — it was an onrushing lorry travelling at over 100mph in our lane, and it was heading straight for our car.

'OH NO!' Samantha screamed.

Impulsively, I swerved my car as quickly as I could to the right. Seconds later, the lorry drove right alongside us and continued off into the distance. We were only moments away from being crushed. Beads of sweat had begun to gather on my forehead and I was breathing heavily. I then parked our car at the side of the road, so we could regroup. Other drivers who had witnessed the incident then began to park behind us. Many were surprised at how we'd managed to avert the crash, and seeing our foreign number plate, sympathised with us. Knowing that we could've been killed if I had reacted only a second slower was daunting, but I was just grateful that we were still alive.

We couldn't make a U-turn, so we took the car all the way to Chelmsford. It was 3pm and now over thirteen hours since we'd left Duisburg. I was completely exhausted and losing my concentration. I decided to contact my Dutch friend, Joachim, if he could provide any help. He was able to call us a cab who led us to his place in Chingford. Samantha, Arouna and I would be staying in Joachim's house until we were able to find a place for ourselves. We'd managed to do it; we were finally in England. But only one question remained: was this *really* the beginning of a new life?

Chapter 21: The Irony of a New life

A year after our arrival in England, Samantha got pregnant and gave birth to our first daughter and second child whom we named after Mary. Two years later, I had my second daughter. A few months after the birth of my second daughter, I made numerous attempts to enrol in university, but all my applications were rejected. I was told I didn't have the right entry requirements to enter university. After receiving the feedback, I wasn't really sure about how to proceed. Did that mean I couldn't get back to school? Thinking about what to do, I decided to visit my local college. Perhaps they could provide me advice on how best I was to proceed. I didn't want anything to stop me from achieving my dreams and fulfilling my promise.

'Hello.'

'Hello sir, how can I help today?'

'Well, I've applied to more than five universities and none of them accepted my application.'

'Oh, I'm sorry to hear that. Why didn't they accept you?'

'They said I lacked the necessary entry requirements and said I should visit my local college for advice.'

After hearing what I had said, the administrator registered me onto Level One Maths and English courses. I was also put on an Access Course, which would provide me the necessary entry requirements. I was 37 years old when I enrolled into Waltham Forest College. For me, it was just a matter of fulfilling my dream of education.

A few days later, I was at college and meeting new friends.

'Hi, my name's Peter.'

'Hi, I'm Chris.'

'Are we the only people here above the ages of 30? Or are there others coming?'

Chris laughed.

'No.'

As more people came, I met Malcolm who was 56 years old, John, Benjamin and Fatima. But most of the people in the class were between 17 and 19 years old. But it didn't feel like we were of different ages. All of us had good rapport and there was always something to joke about.

'Make sure you do your homework and do something extra at home to help you in class,' said Mr Khan.

Mr Khan was our maths teacher. He was very witty and intelligent. He taught maths in a way it was easy to understand. It was great having him. Sometimes, some of us would have extra maths lessons after class and it was great when the younger ones would join John, Chris, Malcolm and I with our work. We made some really good friends.

Liz Arkless was my tutor on the Access to Higher Education Diploma course and always enjoyed it when the class sat quietly for her arrival.

John, Chris, Malcolm and I were friends really quickly. Perhaps you could blame it on our age, but it was great having them beside me. John, Chris and I aimed to continue studying at university, but Malcolm wasn't so sure. He thought he couldn't cope with the stresses at his age. It wasn't an easy task going back to school, especially when you had to contend with work and other family commitments. But I had to make sure that I prioritised certain things to ensure that I got them done.

I spent two years at college, and before my final year was up, I was looking for which university I would apply for. Liz explained how it could sometimes be difficult. Sometimes, you'd really want to go to one university, but they don't accept you. But as the days got closer, I knew I was only a few months from getting to university and achieving my dream. I aimed to study Criminology with Psychology. Liz told me that I only had five choices. After visiting Kingston University on their Open Day, I was really looking forward to getting into that environment. I saw other students of similar age to me also fighting for a place at university. I was rocketed with joy and from then on I knew that I couldn't let the opportunity slip out of my hands. Promptly after visiting other universities, I made my choices: City University London, Kingston, Southbank, Metropolitan and the University of East London (UEL).

City University was my first choice. It was the university I really wanted to go to. After receiving advice from Liz and others, I knew it would be great for me if I got in. I really liked Kingston also, but the distance to travel to university every day was too much, especially from where I lived. Choosing the right university was a huge challenge. I had to find a university, which would not only suit my needs, but also my family's needs and really help me to achieve my goal. In no time, I received offers from all the universities I put down as my choices. The funny thing was that only a few years earlier had I been scouting for the universities that would accept my application, but now I could pick from five. Sadly, however, City University retracted their offer for a reason I was totally unclear of. I told Liz about what had happened, but she told me not to lose heart, that these things happened at times. Nonetheless, I placed Kingston as my first choice, and UEL as my second choice.

I would really have loved to go to Kingston University, but knowing that it would be too far to travel, I decided it was best to attend the UEL. I never planned to attend UEL. In fact, I'd never thought about it until it really came down to the wire. But it had the courses I wanted, and was only fifteen miles away from where I lived. I had finally chosen: UEL would be where I would start my university journey.

Like most other children in England, I was getting ready to start school in September 2009. For me, it was a new adventure, a new start. All I wanted was for Mary to have been alive to see me that day. I was extremely excited and was already looking forward to meeting my new tutors and classmates. After the reasonable journey to University, I arrived. We were asked to sit in a hall where the Module Programme Leader would come in and give a speech on behalf of the staff in the school. His speech was highly encouraging and motivating. The speech boosted my morale and gave me the courage to cope with the pressures of university. I was already looking forward to the first lecture.

My first lecture at university was with Dr Anthony Gunter and it was certainly enjoyable. I was yet to meet my tutor, Professor Daniel Briggs, but was looking forward to it, especially after finding out a lot of people liked his teaching. While attending a lecture in criminology, I met Nathan and both of us were doing the same modules and so it was good to see a familiar face when I went to psychology. I was settling into university life and we were soon in the second semester of my first year. This was the exam period, and I'm sure I didn't know what to expect.

I hated the exam period. It wasn't that I didn't know what to do; it was that sometimes I didn't know the best way to express myself. Sometimes, I'd be able to write exactly what I meant, but at times I couldn't. I was always nervous before an exam and the pressure of that environment never did me any good. For me to clench a pen and put my thoughts to paper, knowing that someone would be reading it and judging what I wrote, was not only terrifying, it was almost crushing my self-esteem. At first, I thought university would be okay. Of course, there would be a few hiccups here and there, but I never recognised that it was going to be as difficult as it was. Although I tried so hard — believe me, I did — I failed one of my modules. The results came on February 17 2010. I could never forget that day, because it hurt. When you put in so much hard work beforehand and you get into an exam, and your brain goes blank — it's hard. I was told that I had to re-sit the module, and that meant another exam at the end of the academic year. It would mean starting from square one and I hated it.

The following month, on 25 March 2010, I was sitting down in the lecture room with Mikhaela, Jurgita, Pascal, and Nathaliya. It was the last lecture before the end of the second semester. Our psychology lecturer, Ian, had told us to get prepared for it the week before. Not really sure what it would involve, I was looking forward to it already. The lecture was on the development of children and cognitive bases of behaviour. At first it was rather interesting, but as the lecture progressed, it got harder and harder to listen. What I saw and what was being said triggered my thoughts. I began to reminisce about my past experiences and what had happened to me when I was younger, but I could hold the pain back no longer. I left the lecture in tears. I stood outside and composed myself. I thought about leaving, but what point would there be? Perhaps, the lecture could help me. At that, I walked back in and listened. When the three hour lecture finished, I was still overwhelmed by my emotions. Although I had stopped crying, the pain of my past was still weighing heavily on my shoulders. I knew that I would get asked questions from my friends and I didn't really want to answer them, so I rushed out of the lecture hall. As I walked towards the exit of the building, I missed my step and my left boot hit my right. I was staggering and completely lost control of myself. I was falling to the concrete ground — head first — when my bag flew over my head and protected my forehead from hitting the ground. I couldn't believe what had happened. My body was shaking and it felt like I was pinned to the ground. Slowly, I lifted myself up and carefully took the journey back home.

I guess it can sometimes prove difficult to cope with the situations that have happened in your past and even though you want to let go, you can't, simply because it's part of you. I still had nightmares, sometimes they were sporadic, and other times they were regular. But after that lecture, I recognised that my past was who I was, my present was who I was becoming and my future was who I was going to be. So even if I tried to, I couldn't really forget. I didn't know whether that made any sense, but neither did some of the events that happened in my life. Perhaps, it was beginning to affect me psychologically; I didn't really know. That was always a familiar tale in my life — not knowing what to do. I just hoped that one day a situation would come when I actually knew.

Whilst I was struggling with my emotions, particularly in my psychology lectures, I was also getting prepared to take my re-sits. I knew I was under pressure. I needed 120 credits to get through my first year, but I only had 80. I didn't think I would have been able to do it, until my tutor, Professor Daniel Briggs, took the opportunity to speak to me.

'It was a pleasure to see you working so hard. You have made big steps this semester, but it doesn't surprise me because you are one of the few students who treat setbacks as challenges, that is you accept them and deal with them positively. You then seek to raise yourself by working extremely hard. Last semester, there was a slight setback but this semester, you have really thrown everything at this course and it is starting to pay off. You have laid solid foundations for next year and I am confident you will get what you deserve and do very well.'

His words were like water to a dying soul. I didn't realise how much faith Daniel had in me, until he spoke to me like that. I was encouraged and motivated to work harder and ensure I succeed in my re-sits. In August 2010, I received my results and thankfully I had achieved the credits I needed. I was grateful to all those who had given me their help and encouragement. Even though I had managed to get through the first year, I was still struggling to manage my emotions.

Just before the lectures would start again in September, I met Iehana, who arranged for me to visit a psychologist on campus after hearing about my experiences. I wasn't sure whether to do it, but perhaps it would help me cope better with university. A few days later, I went to see Mr McCarthy.

'Hello.'

'Hi.'

'My name's John McCarthy. How are you?'

'I'm Peter. I'm good thanks, how are you?'

'I'm good Peter. It must be hard out there and I'm glad you had the courage to talk about your experiences.'

Slightly baffled by how the meeting was going to go, I was surprised by how encouraging and fortifying John was. I told him how sometimes I'd have really bad nightmares, where it would feel that I was passing away in my sleep. Samantha would hear me shouting and screaming and would have to tap me furiously to get me to wake up. I told him I'd sometimes just start crying after reminiscing about my past and how sometimes I found it difficult to cope under pressure. After I narrated to him all that had befallen my life, his words were so comforting and reassuring. It felt like someone understood how I was feeling. At that, I tried to apply his advice about always doing what would make me happy for the rest of the academic year.

We were now in the second semester of my second year at university. So far, it had gone better than my first and I was really enjoying myself. I thought that being a 39 year old mature student at university would mean that finding friends would be somewhat difficult. Surprisingly, it wasn't. I had so many: Eira, Lisa, Mikhaela, Nathan, Natalia, Samuel, Lauren, Dorina, Joyann, Daniela, Cigdem, Alya, Fola, Sylvia, Dimitar and so many more who were just so awesome. I think that's a good word. I could roll the names of my friends off the top of my tongue, until my tongue got twisted. It was great! Although most of them were more than ten years younger than me, I was treated like I was the same age. We all had a really good friendship. Sometimes, we'd go to the pub and have so much fun. And then there was the lecturers and staff: Daniel, who was the self-proclaimed leader of our cohort, always joined us, George — the employability manager — became the pillar of our group, and Fiona, the Commander-in-Chief, I'd like to say (*or Dean of the School of Law and Social Sciences to be more formal*) were always present at our pub parties. The atmosphere and joy on campus was brilliant. Results were up from last year and the mood at our campus was inspiring, until the news came from Matthew…

As I walked through the corridors of UEL's Duncan House Campus, my mind was empty. I was heading for room DH: 001 — the lecture room. I entered and sat quietly by myself at the end of the row. My eyes were brimming and as I tried to control the tears that would run down my cheeks, but my resistance only mattered for a few seconds until I was tapped on the shoulders by Daniel. I explained to Daniel what had happened. Realising that I couldn't take part in the lecture, I was sent home. I then took the time to reflect on what had happened. It had all happened in a matter of days...

'Hello Peter. It's me, Matthew.'

'Oh Matthew, hi. How are you?'

He had interrupted me in the middle of me doing my revision for the next seminar, after returning home from university.

'Is it important?'

'It's very important.'

'Okay, give me a few minutes. I'll call you back.'

A few minutes later, I returned Matthew's call.

'What's up?'

'Things have gone bad.'

'What happened?'

'It's about Mama Cathy.'

'What about Mama Cathy?'

'She had a stroke.'

'Oh my goodness! Is she okay? Have you taken her to hospital?'

'You need to come to Gabon. This is serious.'

'Is she okay?' I asked slowly.

'She's paralysed Peter from her legs down. She can't speak…'

Matthew's voice was fading away, as he nearly began to cry.

'Peter, you need to come to Gabon now.'

'Where is she?'

'She's at home with us. She's under the doctor's supervision.'

This was surreal. This was the woman who had helped me grow up, who took care of me when no one else would. It was silly of me to think she was indestructible, but Mama Cathy never got ill. She never lived a poor lifestyle; she was a healthy woman who always went to the farm. I just couldn't explain how it was a stroke. Like Mary, Mama Cathy was my mother. Although she had not adopted me, she never treated me with any less love than Mary did. She was the last mother I had, and now she was disabled, almost instantaneously.

Those were the tears I carried into the corridors of the Duncan House campus…

A few years back, Mama Cathy had explained to me about how scared she was of her family and the fears she had if something terrible happened to her. She would tell me how her family could kill her, because all they wanted was her property. With that in mind, I simply couldn't accept that the 'stroke' was really a stroke.

In the days that followed, Matthew repeatedly called me telling me how important it was for me to return to Gabon. But I was three weeks away from my final exam; leaving to Gabon would cause me a serious problem. My final exams were on the 9 June. Four days later, I would make the trip to Gabon.

After I told my friends the situation I encountered, I received a lot of help and support. There were so many people who gave me their words of encouragement and support. Wasting little time, I made my trip to Libreville. I made sure that my visit would be a secret, including to Mama Cathy. I didn't want anyone to know I was coming; I wanted to meet everyone surprised.

After returning to Mama Cathy's home, I found her sitting on her bed with Mama Celine — the woman who had first helped translate for me — or as I later found out her name: Celine Nndawa.

'Hello Mama Cathy.'

'Dadada.'

She couldn't speak.

Everything that I had been told, I was seeing for myself and more. Mama Cathy was paralysed completely. She was being fed by Mama Celine, but every time the food went into Mama Cathy's mouth, it would fall out again. It was just like watching a little baby eat. I was completely angry with what I saw. I tried to help Mama Cathy by feeding her myself, but she just couldn't take it. It was either that or it was her form of protest. Perhaps she was trying to tell us something, but being in a state of paralysis, we could never know. I just hoped and prayed that somehow she would recover. We were both rocks in each other's life. I needed Mama Cathy as much as she needed me. And now I had to be there for her. It was tough. Holding back my tears in front of everyone, I went into the room I was to stay in and began to weep. I wept for Mama Cathy and until no more tears could drop. Seeing her in the state she was, was poignant more than anything.

Searching for what really happened to Mama Cathy, I asked Mama Celine a few questions. Mama Celine had accompanied Mama Cathy to the farm. All that happened — I was told — was that Mama Cathy had stepped on something and then fell straight to the ground. But how could everyone have been so sure it was a stroke? I asked if her head had hit the ground and perhaps it was the collision that caused the paralysis, but Mama Celine said that Mama Cathy's head didn't touch the ground. For some reason, the answers I was getting were not satisfactory.

Perhaps no one else could understand it the way I did, but I certainly suspected that Mama Cathy's freak stroke or accident was not so much of an accident. Mama Cathy always said how some of her family preferred her dead so that they could take some of her wealth. She was especially scared of her sister who only lived opposite her; she always saw her as a threat. The abuse she received never disappeared, even well into Mama Cathy's older years. They continued to abuse her and reject her. I guess the oppression never ended when she ran away from home. Personally, I couldn't understand why they hated her so much. Perhaps Mama Cathy was a tough woman, but that's what got her through life. Her resilience, her perseverance, her 'never say never' attitude. It was all this that made Mama Cathy who she was. You couldn't hate someone who tried so hard every day to be a better person. It just didn't make sense to me and I so desperately wondered whether it made any sense to them too. But then again, you always get those people who are just jealous of who are or what you become — the haters per se. Don't you?

I spent a month in Gabon before I returned back to London. Her health progressed a little during the time I was there. She was able to move her arms and sit upright again. I told Matthew to take good care of Mama Cathy and make sure that he gave her the best of his attention. As astutely as my cousin always replied, he gave me his reassurance. I then spoke to Mama Cathy one final time before I would make my way to the airport.

'Mama Cathy, I know you may not be able to answer me, but you can hear me. I want you to know that I love you and I will always continue to love you. You are my mother and I will never forget that. You helped me when I thought I had nothing left to fight for. You gave me a purpose in my life. You gave me so much…I'm so sorry to see you like this and if I could do anything to reverse what has happened to you I would. I love you Mama. But I have to go back to England now and I need you to be strong. I need you to be strong Mama Cathy.'

We were both sitting on the bed. I paused and began to hold her.

'This is a difficult time, I know. But I want you to know that you will be okay. I will make sure we sort this out. I promise that I will do what I can to sort this out. I love you Mama.'

As I departed Mama Cathy, tears began to roll down her cheeks. From then, I knew she had heard me.

The rest of the summer went quite quickly and I was now approaching my third and final year at university. Knowing that I was on Erasmus programme with Sandra, one of my friends, for my final year was great. At least I would have a familiar face to talk to. I was going to be travelling to the Netherlands to study at Utrecht University. I was being given an absolutely extraordinary opportunity and I was already looking forward to it. I knew I would miss my family and a lot of my friends, but it was a great opportunity to visit another country and see how it feels to study. I didn't know what to expect, but I was just excited to get going.

I arrived at Utrecht University on the 1 September 2011. I was directed to a large student hall, where I met Robert and Mario. Funnily enough, they were on the same course as me. We were all international students, so it was great meeting new people from different countries. I collected my keys and then headed to Warande — the university block where I was staying. I then met

Elsa, Alex and Gudise who were my next door neighbours per se. After we were handed maps to tour the city, I went with Gudise to tour the city. We had to figure out a route to get to class every morning so we went on the bus and met different people. Thankfully, the people we met on the streets could speak a little English so it was largely easy to redirect ourselves when we lost our way. A few hours later, Gudise and I went to the university's pre-arranged tour. We also used that opportunity to figure out where everything was. Utrecht was a very large university and it would take me a few weeks to fully understand how to get anywhere without getting lost.

Life at Utrecht University was challenging. Living on my own wasn't hard; it was just that they never had anything I wanted to eat. I would go to the shops late at night in search for anything I could cook, but not only were the prices very expensive, they didn't hold any African delicacies. For many nights, I was stuck with cooking pasta. I guess I was getting the full student experience. Coupled with my lack of satisfactory eating, we were put under immense pressure for seminars and lectures. We were told to read over 300 page books in less than a week in preparation for a mini-test in the next seminar. I spent nights reading and reading and reading. I was always a slower reader than most so I knew I had to work harder and for longer just to make sure I knew it. Although I did enjoy my stay at the World's 48th Best University or perhaps to make it sound better, Europe's 12th Best University (according to the Shanghai Ranking), it was extremely demanding.

After my final exams in January in Utrecht, I returned to England for my final semesters. During this time, several issues began to surface. A few months after I left Gabon, I was told that Mama Cathy's family had been visiting her place to threaten her and take her away from her home. This was despite a doctor telling Mama Cathy's family that they could not move Mama Cathy away because it would affect her recovery and such an action was completely unacceptable. But the desperation to take Mama Cathy's property was growing. They just wanted to have Mama Cathy under their control so that they could do anything that they wanted. Mama Cathy had a lot of properties in Gabon. Her property portfolio was probably worth millions upon millions of CFA francs. I didn't even find out until a few years back, until Mama Cathy told me her fears about her family. So her family's recent action that they wanted to 'take care of her' just didn't add up. They had a vested interest in Mama Cathy, not with her wellbeing but with her wealth. And there was absolutely no way Matthew and I were going to allow them to take her away from her home. But something happened…

On 17 March 2012, Matthew was summoned to the local police station in Lalala Sogatol. The police station was about three miles away from where Mama Cathy lived. The warrant for the arrest of my cousin, Matthew Idowu, was issued by Mama Cathy's family. Now, we were absolutely certain that Mama Cathy's family wanted to have Mama Cathy's property. Mama Cathy's worries had been confirmed. Matthew and his wife had been Mama Cathy's carers, along with Mama Celine so by taking Matthew away it would bolster the claim of Mama Cathy's family that they had to take her away to give her 'better' medical attention. But by taking Matthew, I couldn't help but think that they were trying to get to me. It had all made sense to me a while ago that the nickname Mama Cathy had given to me — mon enfant — was a public declaration that I was her son. And people knew that Matthew was my cousin, so by taking Matthew, they were getting to me.

There was no one else home when Matthew was summoned to the police station so he had to travel with Mama Cathy in the wheelchair all the way to Fopi gendarmerie in Sogatol. The worst thing was that after making the trip, the police then told Matthew that they couldn't proceed with the case because it was a family matter. They tried to interview Mama Cathy, not knowing that she couldn't speak. When she replied with silence, it became clear to the officers in charge that there was no point with proceeding with the case. Palpably, Mama Cathy's family became increasingly frustrated with Matthew. Matthew began pleading for my help, but I didn't know what to do. What could I do? I couldn't leave to Gabon, I was in the middle of school. I had many sleepless nights. We couldn't just let Mama Cathy be taken by her family. Inasmuch as that may sound like the proper solution, the ills and trials they had made Mama Cathy go through were innumerable. It just wasn't fair to let her go. Moreover, they didn't care about Mama Cathy's health; it was more about her wealth.

A few days later, on 24 March, I received a phone call from Matthew very late at night. It was about 11.30pm and I wondered why Matthew was calling me so late.

'Hello Matthew.'

'Hello.'

He sounded apprehensive and he was breathing heavily.

'Are you okay?'

'Mama Cathy's home has been surrounded by police. I've been smuggled to a neighbour's place, but right now they're looking for me.'

'Where's Mama Cathy?'

'She's inside. I had to get out. There was nothing I could do.'

'How long have you been there?'

'Almost twenty minutes, but they're knocking on everyone's houses. It's only a matter of time before they find me.'

'What's all the shouting I'm hearing?'

'There's a huge mob as well. Most of them have machetes and knives. I only have a few minutes.'

The urgency and fright was increasing in every word that he was saying.

'Matthew, they will find you. Make sure you stay low and do not move from where you are. You only have a matter of minutes before they find you.'

'Peter, I'm scared.'

'Matthew, you can't be. You've got to be strong. For Mama Cathy. You've got to be strong.'

The shouting and banging on the doors was getting louder. I knew it would only be a matter of seconds.

'Matthew when they get you, I want you to leave the phone on. Do not switch it off, I want to hear everything that happens.'

Suddenly, the voices get quieter until no further voices can be heard. It sounds like they have left.

'Peter.'

'Yeah.'

'I think they're gone.'

'You can never be too sure. Stay there for a while and then find a way to get out of there. I'll call you back.'

It was so important for Matthew to get out of the area. I knew it would be difficult. The man the mob had come to hunt down hadn't been caught. This was going to be a stake-out. Ten minutes later, I called Matthew back.

'Where are you?'

'I'm still there.'

'Move only when you're ready and sure it's safe.'

'I think so now.'

'Make sure you get out of there. Do not at any cost try to return back to Mama Cathy's place.'

'I'm ready.'

'Put the phone in your hand and keep it with you. I want to hear everything.'

His neighbour leads him out from the back of the building. Matthew has to leave alone, so he doesn't cause suspicion. Suddenly, Matthew shouts, I can hear a struggle. Then, the phone goes dead.

Damn.

At once, I begin to call everyone I know to find out what's happened. After a few hours, I still don't know where he is or what's happened to him. I'm told that Udoh and Bonne-Jean, the children of Mama Cathy's sister living opposite Mama Cathy, were leading the mob.

I was told that they took Mama Cathy from her home. She was screaming and crying, but no one could help her. There was no saviour. As the story was being recounted, I didn't cry. I was more angry — angry that I perhaps hadn't done enough to help her. I just imagined how Mama Cathy must've felt when they took her away from her own home. She would've been defenceless, unable to speak, unable to do anything. Although she would have waved her arms, she was weak. She would've used all her energy to scream and shout, but she could do nothing to stop them. As the mob and police swarmed inside Mama Cathy's home, they kicked out Matthew's wife and threw Matthew's belongings onto the ground outside.

A few minutes after I find out what happens to Mama Cathy, I receive a phone call from Eko to tell me what happened. It was very early in the morning, perhaps 1am, when Matthew decided to leave his neighbour's home. He thought everything was calm and quiet and decided to return home, contrary to what I had told him. He was unaware that his wife had been kicked out, Mama Cathy had been taken, and his clothes were littered on the ground.

Cautiously, he exits from the back of the house and tries to get home. Then, he is gagged and his head smashed against the wall. His head begins to bleed and he struggles to breathe. The person who's holding him calls for the support of his mob who swarm in to begin beating him. He screams and shouts in pain – dying. The police are shouting. Everyone is shouting. There's so much noise; it's impossible for him to hear. He falls to the ground helplessly. The police attempt to move the mob away and tell Matthew to stand up, but he doesn't respond. They move his arms, but he doesn't respond. They hit him again and tell him to get up; Matthew doesn't get up. The police officers then pick him up and carry him to their car. Leaving the mob behind, they drive off into the night.

I had called Matthew's phone tirelessly that night.

It was now 5am in the morning and I hadn't reached him. What had happened to Matthew? Was he dead? Was he alive? I didn't know. For the last time, perhaps in dying hope, I call Matthew's phone. It rings. I sit upright on my chair. For four hours, his phone hadn't rung. Perhaps someone would pick up.

'Hello.'

'Hello. Hello. Who is this? Where's Matthew?'

'Calm down. Calm down.'

'Who are you?'

'You must be Matthew's cousin. He was hiding at my place.'

I exhaled heavily.

'Do you know where he is?'

'No, I have no idea,' she continued. 'He was on the floor, the police surrounded him, picked him up and put him in their car.'

'Do you know how the car looks like?'

'Erm, I couldn't really tell, it was quite late at night.'

'Ah. I don't know what I'm going to do.'

'But I do remember the registration number of the car if that's useful.'

'Oh my goodness! Yes, yes. Give it to me,' I hurriedly ask.

'It's A…Q…5…double 2…8…double A.'

'Let me repeat that to you. A, Q, 5…2…2…8, A, A.'

'Yes, that's correct.'

'I also remember the make of the car.'

'Yes, go ahead.

'It's a Toyota.'

'Thank you so much. Do you know where they might have been headed to?'

'Well, I think they're from the B2 police station somewhere in Libreville. I don't know exactly where. But only they could do an operation like that.'

'Thank you.'

'I hope you find him…'

'Thank you.'

'Alive.'

I held my breath.

'Good luck.'

The phone went dead. It was too overwhelming. Unsure about whether he was alive or not, at least I had some details as to where he might be and some valuable information on the car. I knew it would be difficult to find him, but I wouldn't give up. There was no way I was going to, especially when my cousin's life was involved.

Mama Cathy's family saw Matthew and I as foreigners in their land. Every time Mama Cathy would make a public announcement to everyone that I was her son and everyone saw how bitter her family was. As far as they were concerned, there was no way that I was her son. And they tried to influence all the tenants in the village that Matthew and I did not belong in Gabon. So perhaps their vendetta to get rid of us was much more than just getting Mama Cathy's wealth. Perhaps it stemmed on the fact that they had a prejudice against 'foreigners' or was that a nice way to say 'Nigerians'? I would never know, and frankly, I didn't care. But it all began to make sense when certain phone calls I made to people to help Matthew out were being returned with a big fat no. Ostensibly, they were too scared. But there were still those, and a surprisingly large majority, who believed that Mama Cathy's family had gone too far and were wrong with trying to kick Mama Cathy out of her own home.

At this time, I remembered the advice Ngema had given to me a while ago about the day when Mama Cathy's family would force the issue of taking her and her property.

'Would it not be right if things got too bad to just let her family take her?'

Perhaps Ngema was right. Ngema was a member of Mama Cathy's family, but one of the few and closest friends of Mama Cathy. I remembered in a video that Mama Cathy had recorded a while back telling Ngema to be a father to Matthew and I and to support us in difficult times if she could no longer do it. She narrated how 'wicked' her family were and why she thus wanted

Ngema to support us because they were both from the same family. I also remembered how Mama Cathy lobbied the Gabonese government a few years back warning them about her family and their vendetta. She also tried to seek protection for us in case of the events that were happening. It was just so sad that now it was really happening. Her fears were becoming a reality and it was becoming increasingly difficult to help her, especially now her family had taken full control of her village.

But even though Ngema's advice may have sounded tempting to another person, there was no way I was going to *let* them take Mama Cathy. Even if Mama Cathy hadn't adopted me or she wasn't my biological mother, the love I had for Mama Cathy was the love any child would have for a mother. Mama Cathy was essentially my mother. I'd lost Mary and I didn't want to lose Mama Cathy too. So I couldn't listen to Ngema's advice, because frankly it was drivel. I knew that Mama Cathy would be looking for me to do something anyway, and I couldn't let her down. We were all scared about her condition, especially since she had now been taken by her family. With their behaviour, she may never recover. I just didn't know what to do. But for the moment, I had to find out what happened to Matthew.

Later that day, I found out more information regarding him. He had been locked up in a cell for the night in the police station. He had received no medical treatment and his clothes were drenched in his blood. No one knew whether he was still alive. And if he was I knew there was only a matter of time before things worsened for him in the cell. Most gendarmes in Gabon were not exactly merciful when it came to inflicting pain. Later that afternoon, I received news of people who knew some of the police officers who took Matthew away to B2 police station. I knew then that the only way to get Matthew out of the cell was to get help from the Nigerian authorities, because the Gabonese authorities were not exactly 'friendly' to Nigerians.

Without delay, I called a Nigerian media online social network seeking help. After providing them the information they needed, they quickly put out the story. It began to get shared to the necessary authorities. Before I knew it, Nigerians were sharing it amongst friends. Calling for the intervention of the Nigerian government, the embassy in Gabon intervened. So many people provided their messages of support. It was great to see the solidarity shown in the communities of Nigeria and friends worldwide. Seeing the reactions of people caused me to grow in courage. I also called the Nigerian embassy in Gabon regarding the case to find out whether their intervention was actually true. I was told that someone from the embassy was sent to the police station to investigate the matter.

When the emissary arrived at the police station, Matthew was found locked up in his cell. He was incredibly weak, his clothes had begun to pungently smell and his face was bruised all over. His mouth was swollen and it looked like if he had stayed in the cell for perhaps another day, he would have passed away. Matthew needed urgent medical attention.

The Nigerian emissary spoke to the Colonel in charge of the police station about the actions that happened. According to the Colonel, no details had come to his desk regarding the case. He knew nothing about it, but promised to investigate the officers involved and if discipline was required, justice would take its due course. But for some reason, I wasn't convinced. Did the Gabonese authorities really care that much?

As soon as Matthew was released, he was taken to a secure and safe location unknown to any of Mama Cathy's family. Before he left the police station, Mama Cathy's family warned Matthew and his wife to never set feet on Mama Cathy's place again. That was it. It was finished. Mama Cathy's family had taken what they wanted. It was an extremely tiring, but also an equally frustrating period for me.

I sent letters to the President, Justice Minister—I sent letters to every high authority I could possibly send a letter to. I received no response. If there was anything more I could do within my means, I would do it. The worst feeling in the world is knowing that you did the best you could, but that it still wasn't good enough. I was losing another mother. Was it possible to lose two mothers? Mama Cathy did a lot for me. If it wasn't for her, perhaps I would still be walking on the streets on Gabon in search of a way to survive. I just wondered what would be going through her head. I just didn't want her to think that I'd abandoned her. Because I hadn't and would never do it. I just couldn't get someone to help her. Perhaps someday, I would be able to tell her what happened.

Matthew also suffered a lot because of me. I should have been in Gabon, but he took the pain and the hurt and the suffering that would have been given to me. He was humiliated because he took care for a woman he also knew as his mother. His family suffered also; his child and his wife were treated with the same injustice as he was. Matthew's trial caused me to think long and hard about us as individuals and the course of my life.

To describe my life as a journey is perhaps the easiest way to picture it. I'm setting off on a path, not knowing where exactly it will take me, but knowing where I want to go. I face numerous obstacles along the way — dodging, hiding and escaping — but I continue tirelessly on the path. Sometimes in our lives, we experience pain, suffering and heartache, but these are only emotions that make us better people. We begin to understand ourselves, judge our strengths, attempt to reduce our weaknesses, but all of this only motivates us to improve ourselves every day.

After the ills I faced as a young boy, I thought that stowing away on a ship heading to Europe would be a new start — a new life. But in reality, there is no new life. I have had no new life. Instead, I have built on my strengths, improved my weaknesses and worked harder every day to become a better person today than I was yesterday. I have done what other people do every day of their lives. I am no better than the ordinary man, but I realised only later during my travels across continents that even though there may be no new life, every person can have a fresh beginning. In fact, every new day is a new beginning, where we can choose to redefine our ambitions and dreams. But do we ever choose to? Do we ever see a new day as a new beginning?

We don't have new lives, but we can make fresh starts. It simply requires a little purpose and a little strength in determination. And when we do make those fresh starts, it can feel like we're climbing a mountain to which we will never reach the top. It can feel like the problems of the world are weighing down on our shoulders and it can feel like there is just no way out. But there is an important question that couples a fresh start, which defines whether it really is as new as we want it to be: how far am *I* prepared to make it work?

My life from as long as I can remember has been about survival. Something would always happen that would change the route to my destination or make me feel a certain way, but I knew I had to keep on going — it was almost the irremovable urge to get to my destination. Yet, even though I've probably been fortunate in some parts of my life and I've survived to tell my story, it just proved what I knew all along: *a dream is never achieved by the man who stands still, but the one who tries is at least a step closer.*

Me (far right) standing in front of the demolished block factory

Me in Morocco, Casablanca Mohammed V Airport

Me (left) and Singh (right) holding Arouna

Chef Volker (left) and Samantha (right)

Me (far right) washing the dishes at Albert's restaurant

Tai

Me (left), Chris (centre) and Malcom (right) at the graduation ceremony at Waltham Forest College

Me (left), Mama Cathy (centre) and Josephine (right) in Libreville

Elsa (far left), Me (second from left), Claire (front), Alex (far right) at Utrecht University

Me at Utrecht University

Epilogue

A few years after I left Gabon, Jibé left to return to his home in the Democratic Republic of Congo.

Fefe is still in contact with me and our friendship has continued to age.

In February 2007, Arouna and I visited Mama Cathy in Gabon. Arouna was only three months old when he and Samantha left in 1998, so the joy in her face was unbelievable. It was a surprise visit and she loved it very much.

Matthew is still living in Gabon. He's married to a Gabonese woman and they've both been blessed with two children.

Jessica left Gabon, and migrated to her home in Equatorial Guinea.

I was unable to ever find Yanke, Texan, Kofi and Matthew again. But I will always remember them.

I was also unable to locate Lemmy.

I never saw Kate again, but I still have the photos that she hid in my jumper today.

I have met with my half-brothers and sisters since leaving Nigeria, but not all of them have really warmed to me. I also met Jude, one of Elizabeth's children from before she had married Tony, but I am yet to meet her eldest child, Maria.

As for Vincent and Joy, they continue to live in Nigeria, although life has not treated them well entirely. Joy visited me in England in March 2006, after I hadn't seen her for almost 17 years. She visited me for about six months and we talked over a lot of things that had happened.

Samantha and I have been blessed with three children — one boy and two girls. Samantha also became a Jehovah's Witness. It hasn't been easy living a happy married life, especially since the early troubles we encountered in our marriage, but we have worked hard together to educate our children onto the right path.

Jean, M'bembi's father, died in April 2008 following an illness. As for M'bembi, she still lives in Gabon and has been blessed with two children. Since our last encounter in 1998, life hadn't exactly gone smoothly for her. In her own words, she briefly recounts her life:

Peter was my first love. I wanted to marry him, but my father opposed it. As a result, Peter married another woman with whom he has had three children. His wife gave birth to Arouna in Gabon. One day, Peter brought him to our place of worship. That day, I felt like I was being ridiculed and wounded. I left like trash, but I had to keep my calm. At the end of the service, I held the baby in my arms. But I couldn't help but think that I was holding the baby of the one I loved and he was not mine.

A few years later, and in a rush, I fell in love with another man, who is today the father of my two children. I married outside of the faith against my father's wish. It was not necessarily revenge in my eyes, but a statement against the fact that I had lost the love of my life. The living proof of this is what I've suffered as the result of my father's actions.

I regret that the man I thought I loved was only with me as a statement, and in essence to him I am only a superficial woman.

At this moment, I cry so much and regret that my father is no longer alive to see the consequences of his actions. I find it hard when I'm asked to recall my past. I doubt I can love anyone again in the same way I loved Peter. But my message to parents who may be reading this is that my testimony and history should serve as a living lesson.

I appeal to all parents to allow their children to speak their heart and their desires. Love is a great thing if it happens between two people who truly love each other. Only guide your children, do not dictate their lives.

As for Tony, we've had a good relationship since I left Nigeria and I'm glad I was able to see him again in May 2014. He's now 100 years old. Beki did return to Tony's home, but was unable to survive for long. Beki passed away in October 2012, only a few days after returning to Tony's home.

Sadly, Mama Cathy couldn't recover from her stroke. She passed away in her home on 15 December 2013 at the age of 70 and was buried five days later. A few weeks after her burial, government officials came looking for Mama Cathy in order to resolve her case and take her out of the hands of her family. Regrettably, after hearing of her death, they walked away.

So what happened to me? I started my first official job with Pahek Security Services in Nigeria as a security guard, working at a cocoa warehouse. I'd had my first job at 15, and only a year before I dropped out of school. At first, I thought my security job was just something I needed the money for. But I hadn't realised that by working with Pahek, I had set off my career in security.

16 years later, in 2002, I applied for a security job with Amour Security in the UK, where I was employed as a security officer. Two years later, I opened my own security company with a partner. Within a few months, our annual turnover was in five figure sums.

By the end of the year, the company was growing even faster than I'd imagined. The company served some very important clients and I established deep rooted connections with the police force. During the time, I worked as the operations manager of the company and delegated responsibilities to others. I especially remember after only a few weeks of opening my company, I was invited to a members' meeting for the British Security Industry Association. I was sitting down at a round table with Dr Yilkyes Bala, Armour Group Security's director. The irony of it all was that he had no clue that only a few years earlier I had been employed in his company working in the London Borough of Ealing. Now I was sitting with some of the biggest CEOs and directors in the industry.

But during the periods between 2007 and 2008, the recession hit the company hard and we underwent numerous transformations. Knowing that I still hadn't fulfilled my dream of education and my promise to Mary, I took the opportunity to withdraw from full-time work. I became a part-time security manager and began to concentrate on my educational goals.

I never saw working in the security industry as *work* per se. It was something I enjoyed doing and still do today. If it could be my hobby, it was my hobby. If it could be my therapy, it was my therapy. I enjoyed meeting new people every day from various backgrounds. In my professional work, I guess I've been privileged enough to work at a senior management level.

Even though I had all the managerial experience, I didn't have the degree to compliment it. Consequently, I knew I could use the opportunity to further my education and compliment my security profile.

While I was studying my degree at the University of East London, I created the school's first fully fledged Law and

Criminology Students' Society in 2010. My main focus was to create a platform where students could be empowered and explore their future potential. In the beginning, like anything, it was difficult to get students involved. I remember standing at seminars and lectures, telling others my experience and why it was important for them to join. I remember my first stall at UEL's Freshers' Fair. Essentially, it was me at a desk with a few leaflets, and speaking to people to join.

Little did I know then that this society would become the largest society in UEL boasting more than 200 members and lasting for over three years — a University record. Competing with more than 60 other societies, we would also win numerous awards and prizes. The Law and Criminology Students' Society became the only society to have had nine Vice-Presidents in a single academic year, to have continued for more than 1 year and attract some of the most influential persons in the UK (including Grace Ononiwu, Chief Crown Prosecutor- East of England).

The LCSS, as the society's name became abbreviated, enjoyed unparalleled success. In 2010/2011, I won the Gold Award for Society Organiser of the Year; the society won the Gold Award for the Overall Best Society of the Year and the Silver Award for the New Society of the Year. That year I also won a Gold Award for Outstanding Contribution to Volunteering, which was presented to me by Volunteering England.

The following academic year, 2011/2012 (my final year at the university), the society won a Gold Award for the Overall Best Society of the Year and a Bronze Award for Event of the Year. We had won the Gold Award for Overall Best Society of the Year two years running. It was a great achievement.

When I left in 2012, I intended to keep a legacy for the society. I had learnt that as the presidents of societies moved on at the university, the societies closed down. There was no way that was going to happen with the LCSS. So I ensured that after my departure as President of the LCSS, there was another person in waiting. Thankfully, the legacy of the society continues today and we should be the oldest society in UEL's Student Union.

Today, in and amongst the charitable work I do and my position as a part-time security manager in a company, I work on Bond Street at Sotheby's as a security guard. For me, working as a guard was never about the money, I enjoyed doing it. It was almost therapy for me. It took my mind of the things that worried me and I'm able to get involved in a lot of exercise as a result. I liked helping people and being at the frontline just pleased me, as weird as that may sound.

One day, I was working at Sotheby's when my new friend Salvo came up to me. We started talking and I explained a lot about myself. He was very interested in my experience and without hesitation bought the first part to my book. A few days later, Salvo's friend Chris, also bought a copy of my book. The following day, so many staff working at Sotheby's wanted a copy of my book; some of them I hardly spoke to. In the end, I sold a shedload of copies of my first book at Sotheby's. I went there to work and instead I was selling books to everyone.

I'm also an author. I spend most of my time analysing political violence and writing articles about human security. Additionally, I spend some of my time volunteering for LASALA Foundation, a charitable organisation created by myself to help other children who were just like me.

At the moment, I'm enjoying my life per se. It's been a long journey to get to where I am today, but I'm glad to say that it was worth the wait. What next for me? I'm not sure; we'll just have to wait and find out. Sorry, not wait. The journey of a thousand miles begins with a step…

'If you think you can achieve your dreams: go for it! But if you can't, then you're *probably* right.'

Oluwafemi Senu, March 2011 LCSS Conference

On 20 July 2012, I graduated with a Bachelor of Arts with Second Class Upper Division Honours, having followed an approved Honours Programme in Criminology with Psychology.

Following the successful completion of my undergraduate programme, I proceeded with a Master's of Science programme at Kingston University, where I graduated on 15 November 2013 in Terrorism and Political Violence.

Promise fulfilled. Dream achieved.

Arouna (left), Mama Cathy (centre) and me (right) sitting on the dining table in Gabon, 2007

Mama Cathy sitting in Gabon, 2007

Samantha today

M'bembi today

Tony in October 2002

Tony (left) and me (right) in May 2014

Me (third from left) receiving awards with the Law & Criminology Students' Society

Back: Dimitar (left to right), Muhammad, Dorina, Agnieszka, Professor Briggs; Front: Cigdem (left to right), Melissa and me at a meeting for the Law & Criminology Students' Society

Samuel (left to right), Alya, Ivana, Cigdem, Professor Briggs, me, Adaeze

Grace Ononiwu, Chief Crown Prosecutor - East of England (left) and me (right)

Me (left) receiving the Gold Award for 'Outstanding Contribution to Volunteering' from a representative from Volunteering England (right)

Arouna (left) and me (right) receiving the Outstanding Achievement Award for Adult Learners presented by Birbeck University of London and the University of East London

Stewart (left) and me (right) at the Kingston University Masters Graduation Ceremony

Me (left) and my good friend Salvo (right) working together on Bond Street at Sotheby's

PRICE: **£12.99**
ISBN: **978-1-907783-08-1**

ABOUT THE BOOK

In 1971, Elizabeth died and left her seven-month-old baby behind. Fifteen years later, her son discovered the hidden secret, and ran away from home with a ship heading to Europe. Would he survive? Mary was abandoned too and she died mysteriously.

The Unexpected Truth is a remarkable true life story. Elizabeth's son was misfortunate and was struggling to survive. Although he is now living in the UK, his story has not finished and he hopes to live again to complete his mission.

His life story is a journey that was at times painful and difficult, but one he gradually survived, knowing that part of his desire was always in the midst of less privileged children.

AUTHOR'S NOTE

Please bear in mind that I wrote *The Unexpected Truth* without a formal basis of education. I left school at 14, and even when I was in school, I did not pay particular attention in class. My English was not very good, as it was not my first language and I always struggled to convey myself the way I wanted to. When I arrived in the UK, I had to attend Maths & English classes in order to improve my English. So, please bear with me when reading this book. It is a personal story, written from the heart.

I hope this book inspires you to pick up a pen and tell your story one day too. But most importantly, I hope it inspires the younger generation to fulfil their potential.

www.ingramcontent.com/pod-product-compliance
Ingram Content Group UK Ltd.
Pitfield, Milton Keynes, MK11 3LW, UK
UKHW021052270726
13967UKWH00012B/584

9 781907 783098